LENT + EASTER

© 2022 Elane O'Rourke & Benton Stokes
School For Seekers, Inc.
www.schoolforseekers.com
All rights reserved.

ISBN: 978-1-957181-02-8

ABOUT US

ELANE O'ROURKE is a spiritual mentor, teacher, and researcher, with years of pastoring and professoring informing her worldview. She specializes in making sense of difficult ideas and listening for what the Spirit is doing in your life.

BENTON STOKES is a worship leader, songwriter and recording artist whose songs are spiritually intelligent and emotionally relevant. As our Resident Creative he specializes in real life, intimate prayer, and making the ordinary beautiful.

OUR PEOPLE ARE smart, curious, post-evangelical, progressive, agnostic, creative, eloquent, awkward, LGBTQ+ and justice-allied. We are sex-positive, body-positive, spirit-positive and Spirit-positive.

WE CREATED SCHOOL FOR SEEKERS in 2014 to give Christian misfits—usually former evangelicals and political liberals—a place to heal and grow in their relationships with themselves, God, and others.

WE EXPLORE SPIRITUAL LIFE through a wide-angle Trinitarian lens, starting from one truth: God loves and accepts us all and desires relationship with each of us.

WE COMPANION AND LEAD through programs like *17 Embraceable Ideas (that will reconstruct your faith and transform your life)* and *Reading The Bible As If It Matters*, along with life-affirming spiritual direction and coaching.

OUR PODCAST is *Cocktail Theology*, where we talk about life, God, sex, religion, music, roller coasters (both physical and emotional), and anything else that matters, with no filters. We also enjoy a cocktail while we chat (like most of our listeners). You can find it wherever you listen to podcasts.

HOW TO USE THIS BOOK

You could read each day's entry while stopped at a red light, or waiting in line, or bored at work. We don't recommend that approach.

If you want to grow, or heal, or know God and yourself better, this is what we suggest.

Schedule 15 minutes each day. Put it on your calendar. Set an alarm if you need to.

Have a journal and a pen at hand. Physically writing your responses stimulates your brain to retain the ideas and begins to create the new neural pathways that can lead to change.

You may want to light a candle or make a cup of tea. Take in the scent, warmth, taste, sounds; keep engaging your body and mind together.

Begin with 3 deep breaths, followed by a set prayer (see next page for some possibilities).

Following each reflection is a thought question or a prayer suggestion or a practice. Take 5-10 minutes to write in your journal: answer the questions, rewrite the prayer, make a plan to try the practice.

If you find the reflection challenging, try not to argue with it. Instead, try on the ideas that bother you, asking "how would my life be different if I believed this?"

Close with that day's prayer, or a set prayer, or a free prayer of your own.

Take 3 more deep breaths.

Repeat daily.

A NOTE ABOUT THE NUMBERING OF DAYS

Unlike the other seasons of the Christian calendar, Lent and Easter always have the same number of days, which makes keeping track of what day you're on a lot easier than during the rest of the year.

Here's why it can get wonky.

The Christian calendar is based on the Jewish lunar calendar. Lunar calendars don't match the now-standard Gregorian calendar in which some months have 31 days, others 30 or fewer.

Two holy days of the Christian calendar—Maundy Thursday and Pentecost—started as Jewish holy days, so correspond tidily with a lunar calendar.

Christian calendars have one holy day that is fixed by the Gregorian calendar instead of the lunar calendar: Christmas. We celebrate Christmas on December 25, regardless of what the lunar calendar is doing.

The only seasons of the Christian calendar that have a fixed number of days are the seasons of Christmas (12), Lent (46), and Easter (49). Lent begins on Ash Wednesday, which in 2022 is March 2. In 2023 Ash Wednesday falls on February 22, and in 2024 it'll roll around on February 17.

We'll see you then!

—EOR + BKS

SOME SET PRAYERS TO TRY

MORNING

I will sing of your strength in the morning; I will sing of your love. You are my fortress, my refuge in times of trouble. O my Strength, I sing praise to you, O loving God.

Holy and everlasting Father, thank you for bringing me to this new day. Preserve me with your mighty power, that I may not fall into sin, or be overcome by adversity, and in all I do direct me toward the fulfillment of your Kingdom, through Jesus Christ my Lord (*or, through the power of your holy names*), Amen.

EVENING

O God, thank you for the blessings of the day that is past. Bring me and those I love safely to the morning hours so we may rise and enjoy your presence again. Amen.

O gracious light, pure brightness of the everliving Father in heaven, O Jesus Christ, holy and blessed! As we come now to the setting of the sun, and our eyes behold the vesper light, we sing your praises, O God: Father, Son, and Holy Spirit. You are worthy at all times to be praised by happy voices, O Son of God, O Giver of life, and to be glorified through all the worlds.

ANYTIME

Oh Lord, open my lips and my mouth shall declare your praise. Praise Father, Son, and Holy Spirit, both now and forever. The God who was, who is, and is to come at the end of the ages.

Our Father in heaven, may your name be considered holy. May your Kingdom come, your will being done on earth as it is in the heavens. Give us today what we need for today. As we forgive our debtors, forgive us. Do not lead us through times of trial; deliver us through evil. For the Kingdom and the power and the glory are yours, now and forever.

Lent

ASH WEDNESDAY

> As for mortals, their days are like grass; they flourish like a flower of the field; for the wind passes over it, and it is gone, and its place knows it no more. —Psalm 103:15-16

One day, I will die and so will you. Those who love us will mourn as we go on to whatever life looks like after death.

I don't spend a lot of time thinking about the afterlife. I believe the days I'm given are meant to be lived with purpose, going about the work of the Kingdom. I also believe they are to be lived fully—savoring moments, finding joy, and spreading light.

Psalm 103 and other Scripture passages (I'm looking at you, Ecclesiastes!) point to how life begins and ends without fanfare. Most of us don't end wars, cure cancer, or save the planet singlehandedly. Most of us live quietly, exhaling when we can, parenting the best we know how, gambling on big and small decisions, and managing our sometimes- meager resources.

We may do this without much introspection. We may count survival as success. And when we're going about the business of life, that may be all we can manage.

But during Lent, we are invited to ask the hard questions. How do my choices impact my kids? How am I making the world better? What do I do with my one gone-like-grass life?

Truth is, our days are full of ellipses and question marks. Few answers are as pat as we'd like them to be.

So for these next six weeks, my attention goes to the unresolved.

What are your hard questions? Let's ask them together.

—BKS

THURSDAY OF THE FIRST WEEK OF LENT

> By the sweat of your face you shall eat bread until you return to the ground, for out of it you were taken; you are dust, and to dust you shall return. —Genesis 3:19

Adam had it made in the Garden. He was in close communion with God, who loved him dearly and entrusted him with caring for Eden. God had given him a life without pain or disappointment—essentially heaven on earth.

But in a moment, all that changed. Adam did not trust that God would care for Eve and him, and chose instead to trust the serpent. From that moment forward, Adam would eat only if he worked hard. Like digging-ditches-in-Mississippi-in-August hard. Then one day, he would die and return to the dust from which he was made. The end.

Things we do, and think, and think about doing, basically fall into two categories—life-giving and life-destroying. Sins are the acts and attitudes that destroy life—ours or someone else's—and breach relationships.

What Adam did was life-destroying. When I choose the fruit of the forbidden tree, and I have, I am choosing sin. And sin has consequences in this life, not just when I die. My relationships suffer because I put myself first. My hope dries up and the faith life I show the world is smoke and mirrors. Sin is bad.

Now I'm not a legalist. I'm not going to define what sin is for you, even though I think we could agree on some of the big ones. The most dangerous sins are the insidious ones that creep into our behaviors with barely a notice.

During Lent, one of the things we are called to do is deal with the sin in our lives that we brush aside, or pretend isn't there, or wish wasn't there.

—BKS

What is the sin in your life you aren't calling out?

FRIDAY OF THE FIRST WEEK OF LENT

> Many times he delivered them, but they were rebellious in their purposes, and were brought low through their iniquity. Nevertheless he regarded their distress when he heard their cry. For their sake he remembered his covenant, and showed compassion according to the abundance of his steadfast love.
> —Psalm 106:43-45

Sin has consequences.

I know that sentence by itself is something you'd see lit up on a billboard beside an interstate in south Alabama. But it's true. (And I'm not talking about hell. That's a subject for another day.)

What I mean to say is this: when we choose to act in ways that are life-destroying, life is destroyed. Joy is traded for sorrow. Peace for unrest and conflict. Love for self-worship.

God has saved us from ourselves more times than we can count. When our actions have brought us low, God has heard our cries for help and has shown us compassion. Why? Because God has an abundant, steadfast love.

God does not give up on us, even when we act in life-destroying ways.

I've felt the elephant of guilt sitting on my chest because of sin. I've lied to cover up or excuse what I've done. I've avoided the calls and texts from concerned friends.

But I've never had God turn away from me, even when I've turned away from God and everyone else. It isn't in God's nature to do that to me, or to you.

—BKS

What are the consequences of sin you're living with? Why haven't you cried out to God? Or, if you have, what have you heard back?

SATURDAY OF THE FIRST WEEK OF LENT

Nathan said to David, 'You are the man! Thus says the Lord, the God of Israel' —2 Samuel 12:7a

Nathan was King David's advisor and trusted friend. He was also a prophet, which means he was a truth teller.

In 2 Samuel 12, Nathan came to share a story with David about a rich man with many herds and a poor man who had nothing but a cherished lamb. When a traveler came to the rich man's home, instead of taking one of his countless sheep to feed his guest, the rich man took the poor man's beloved lamb.

Upon hearing this, David was outraged, saying the rich man should repay the poor man fourfold and be sentenced to die for this injustice. But Nathan was quick to point out that David was the rich man in the story, taking Bathsheba from her husband, Uriah, and then ordering Uriah killed (*see 2 Samuel 11*).

God had blessed David beyond measure, but David still took what wasn't his to take.

We take things that don't belong to us. When we gossip, we take someone's good reputation. When we cheat to win, we take someone else's victory. When we lie, we take away the ability of others to recognize truth.

Why do we do it? We take because we think that what we have isn't enough. Instead of celebrating God's many blessings with life-giving joy, we diminish what we have and desire what others have with life-destroying envy.

Do you have a Nathan in your life? You know, that friend who can tell you the truth, even when you don't want to hear it? David was able to hear the hard truth from Nathan because he knew Nathan loved him.

God uses those people in our lives to show us where we've mis-stepped, what we need to do to make it right, and how to avoid those life-destroying actions and attitudes going forward.

—BKS

Do you have someone who's willing to tell you the truth...and from whom you can hear it?

SUNDAY OF THE FIRST WEEK OF LENT

> Other seeds fell on good soil and brought forth grain, some a hundredfold, some sixty, some thirty. —Matthew 13:8

The Parable of the Sower paints a simple picture. A sower drops seeds. Some land on the path and get eaten by birds. Some land in shallow soil, take root quickly, then burn up in the day's heat. Some land in thorns, where their growth is strangled. And some land in fertile soil and grow to produce lots of grain.

The important takeaway for us in this parable from Jesus is how important it is that we prepare the soil of our souls and spirits.

That's what spiritual disciplines are for. It's why we make a practice of praying, reading the Bible, choosing the longest line at the grocery store, letting someone else have the final word, and so on.

Tending to our spiritual soil takes attention and lots of work. But all the effort that we (and Jesus, as we will see later in Lent) put into preparing our soul-soil is worth it because of the connection it builds between us and God. And once our soil is fertile, we aren't usually even aware when God sows a seed.

—BKS

What are you doing during Lent to prepare your soil for the seed God wants to sow?

MONDAY OF THE FIRST WEEK OF LENT

For I do not do the good I want, but the evil I do not want is what I do. Now if I do what I do not want, it is no longer I that do it, but sin that dwells within me. —Romans 7:19-20

Old habits are hard to break. That's because they get into our muscles if not our bones. Habits so completely take over our bodies that our minds don't even notice we have them. That's why willpower doesn't work: most of the time we do something we aren't even aware we're doing it.

So when we want to change something about ourselves, we have to start by noticing our troublesome habits and then work to form new, healthier ones.

That's what spiritual practices help us do. The life-destroying actions and attitudes we form over time don't change just because we will them to. The inner back-and-forth of Romans 7 is the internal struggle we all face: we want to do good and refrain from what's not good, but longstanding habits pull us right back.

There's the kind of person I want to be—patient, self-denying, kind, and compassionate. And then there's the person I am. But I can retrain my mind and body by taking on a spiritual practice, like choosing to drive in the slow lane in order to become more patient, or fasting from something I typically am quick to indulge in to practice self-denial. Spiritual practices use our bodies to change our minds.

During Lent, one of the things we do is follow Jesus into the desert, where he fasted, prayed, and faced his own temptations. Yes, even Jesus had to be intentional about focusing his mind and body on God. That's why he practiced solitude, and self-denial, and spent time with God: he was retraining his body to change his mind.

In the same way, we build our own spiritual stamina through practice and prayer, becoming more and more like Jesus as we do.

—BKS

What spiritual practice(s) are you taking on during Lent to retrain your body and mind?

TUESDAY OF THE FIRST WEEK OF LENT

> The righteousness of the righteous shall be his own, and the wickedness of the wicked shall be his own. —Ezekiel 18:20b

By the time of the prophet Ezekiel, the Israelites already knew that the consequences of failing to follow God's commands was death. God speaks through Ezekiel, detailing the actions that are considered righteous—things like being just, caring for the poor, and not worshiping idols. No surprises there: the Israelites had heard all of it before.

But before that moment, fathers and sons were punished for one another's sins. If a father committed a wrong act, his sons and their sons could also be punished. In Ezekiel 18, God says something startling: No one would be penalized for sins committed by someone else.

And then, God goes on to say this, When the wicked turn away from the wickedness they have committed and do what is lawful and right, they shall save their life (v. 18:27). God offers the Israelites a chance to commute any death sentence they've earned, by changing their ways.

When we acknowledge our life-destroying behaviors and attitudes and then choose a different path, God offers us abundant life. Making different choices means forming new, life-giving habits. Forming those habits requires spiritual exercise, just like learning a new physical skill requires physical exercise.

Spiritual practices shape habits over time, and turn us from our old, life-destroying ways that affect far more people than just ourselves.

—BKS

What life-destroying actions and intentions do you see in yourself? What spiritual practices might help you form new life-giving behaviors instead?

WEDNESDAY OF THE SECOND WEEK OF LENT

> Create in me a clean heart, O God, and put a new and right spirit within me. —Psalm 51:10

In the living of our lives, we pick up stains: the marks of harm we experience and inflict.

Without thinking we retreat into ourselves and away from God.

We get used to destructive opinions and ways of speaking, things like sarcasm, unkindness, and conspiracy-chasing. They shape our thoughts so subtly we don't see it happening.

We destroy others and ourselves in little ways, through neglect, or shame, or arrogance, bit by bit.

Over time all those small errors and lapses take us off course, and sometimes we don't even realize by how far.

"Create in me a clean heart," David prays, after his friend Nathan makes him aware of how he has wronged God and others by taking Bathsheba for himself. Over time, his attitudes and actions had shaped him into a man who would steal another man's wife. His heart had been stained by thoughts and habits he hadn't even realized he had.

David goes to God, pleading for mercy, confessing what he has done, and asking to be restored. In fact, the word create that David uses in verse 10, is the same word used in Genesis 1. David is asking God to literally create his heart all over again.

Maybe you've been shaken by the shoulders after a season of self-absorbed behavior.

I know I have.

Our stained hearts keep us from the closeness we were always meant to have with God. When we move away from God, it's rarely a single, decisive act. It happens one small choice at a time. That's why it is up to us to change what we're doing, to act decisively and consistently to restore the closeness we long for.

—BKS

What life-destroying behaviors have crept into your life? How will you address them in order to draw closer to God?

THURSDAY OF THE SECOND WEEK OF LENT

Where can I go from your spirit? Or where can I flee from your presence? —Psalm 139:7

I knew from an early age that God was always around.

As a teenager, I understood that to mean God was watching. Closely. And taking notes. That God was the kind of Father you can run from, but you can't hide from.

Later, as I discovered God outside the church of my youth, I came to see God as present ... but also kind of detached, like there were more important matters to tend to than me.

Then when my internal conflicts around faith and sexuality became too big to keep burying, I began to experience God's presence as a source of security and peace. Even when my world was unfamiliar and uncomfortable, God was familiar and close. Despite what I'd been taught, and even what I was feeling, I knew that I was truly seen, fully known, and wonderfully made.

The Psalmist David says God knit me together in my mother's womb and that in God's book were written all the days that were formed for me, when none of them as yet existed.

God knows our thoughts, our ways, and the words we don't speak.

That's why trying to hide from God is fruitless, frustrating, and life-destroying. God sees and knows everything about us, and yet continues to cherish us and desire our company.

We can't flee from God's presence—and why would we want to?

—BKS

Recall a time when you tried to hide from God. What did you discover about yourself and about God?

FRIDAY OF THE SECOND WEEK OF LENT

And I heard a loud voice from the throne saying, 'See, the home of God is among mortals. He will dwell with them; they will be his peoples, and God himself will be with them'
—Revelation 21:3

Like the *Lord Of The Rings* books of JRR Tolkien? Read *Revelation*. It's full of wild, cryptic imagery and apocalyptic weirdness. In this passage, Revelation's writer (John) sees an actual city dropping out of the sky—and that's one of the less shocking events he describes.

Many people read this passage as John predicting the future arrival of a new Jerusalem. But that's not what was happening: John was seeing it happen in real time and recording what he saw as best he could. What he is describing is already there, then. And here, now.

The truth is the kingdom of God has coexisted with our own personal kingdoms, albeit uncomfortably, since Eden. The kingdom is here now, and much of the time we feel it as a threat to what we want. We've stood up to the Almighty over and over again, beating our chests and demanding our way.

As a result, our world isn't free from mourning, crying, pain, and death. Instead we have a climate crisis, crippling poverty, deep racial divides... you get the picture. Nevertheless, the home of God—the new Jerusalem—is and has been with us all along. God lives among us, dries our tears, makes things new.

The reconciliation John saw is already at work. The question we face is whether we will make the life-giving choice to be a part of it.

As people of God, we can stay safe and comfortable in God's steadiness while the problems of humanity rock our planet. Or we can seek out a life in God's kingdom now, working to bring hope, peace, and light to the darkness around us.

—BKS

What are you doing to help bring reconciliation to your world?

SATURDAY OF THE SECOND WEEK OF LENT

> For in him all the fullness of God was pleased to dwell, and through him God was pleased to reconcile to himself all things, whether on earth or in heaven, by making peace through the blood of his cross. —Colossians 1:19-20

Want to know how God would treat a woman with a regrettable reputation who was being harassed and humiliated by religious men? Look at how Jesus treated her (*John 8:7*).

Ever wonder how God feels about the poor, the meek, and the powerful? Jesus talked about that (*Matthew 5:3*).

The point is, we know God, at least in part, because we know Jesus.

In Jesus' actions, we see God's character, compassion, and heart for humanity.

In Jesus' words, we hear what is most important to God, and how God would say it.

In Jesus' life, we see modeled for us the kind of life God desires us to live.

God's fullness dwelled in Jesus.

But we also believe that Jesus was fully human, so we must accept that he was as capable as we are of making mistakes, choosing wrongly, and even abandoning his calling.

I mean, I've not always been faithful to God. Have you? But because Jesus was, I believe I can be. The fact that I can see both myself and God in Jesus gives me tremendous hope. I am reconciled to God through Jesus.

—BKS

What do you believe about Jesus' divinity? His humanity? How do your views affect the way you live your Christian life?

SUNDAY OF THE SECOND WEEK OF LENT

And the Word became flesh and lived among us, and we have seen his glory, the glory as of a father's only son, full of grace and truth. —John 1:14

I'm a songwriter. I love crafting a new lyric from bits of experience, knowledge, and perspective that I've acquired here, there, and everywhere, and then finding a way to make the words sing. I know it's one of the things God made me to do.

I also know that God is creative too. In John 1, we read "All things came into being through him, and without him not one thing came into being" (v. 3). So when I read verse 14, I find it both bizarre and wonderful that God would become one of us, a product of God's own imagination.

It would be like me becoming a song I'd written. Might be fun to be in somebody's 'spiritual-but-not-crazy' playlist. Still...seriously weird. I think God knew it was weird too, but that's the mystery of intimacy between God and us.

Here's something else: the word for lived used here means pitched a tent. Imagine being at Coachella and God pitches a tent next to yours, offers you an IPA, and recalls a favorite Led Zeppelin concert where Jimmy Page first played that solo in Stairway To Heaven. Sounds ridiculous, but that is pretty much what God did. And does.

As we start recognizing the voice of God in Jesus' words, and seeing the heart of God in Jesus' actions, God become less abstract, less untouchable, more like us.

—BKS

Where do you notice God in your present circumstances?

MONDAY OF THE SECOND WEEK OF LENT

And have them make me a sanctuary, so that I may dwell among them. —Exodus 25:8

I enjoy home renovation shows. You know, where a less-than-desirable house gets a makeover, and then there's a big reveal for the homeowners. There's typically minimal drama (*It's the wrong shower head!*), and everyone is happy in the end.

My current favorite home-reno show is called *Home Town*. The interior designer and her woodworker husband bring old bungalows and farmhouses back to life, adding in awww-inspiring family photos, meaningful heirlooms, and lots of Southern charm. They seem to understand that it takes more than thoughtfully placed pretty things to create a home where someone can live happily ever after.

In Exodus 25, God asks Moses to collect precious things from the Israelites to use in the building of a sanctuary for God. Things like gemstones, leather and skins, precious metals, acacia wood, oils, and incense from all whose hearts prompt them to give (*v. 2*).

None of these items would've been hiding forgotten in a box in the attic. These were things of value, handled with great care and displayed proudly. To part with them would be like giving up your *Action Comics #1*, or the keys to your 1965 Camaro, or your grandmother's diamond earrings.

Truth is, God doesn't want our precious things. And God doesn't need a nice place to come home to.

What God wants is to dwell with us, and in us. We give God a home when we offer ourselves. And we make that home beautiful by becoming the people God desires us to be.

—BKS

What of yourself—mind, body, soul, spirit, will, environment—are you willing to give to God?

TUESDAY OF THE SECOND WEEK OF LENT

> Let no foreigner who is bound to the Lord say, 'The Lord will surely exclude me from his people.' And let no eunuch complain, 'I am only a dry tree.' For this is what the Lord says: 'To the eunuchs who keep my Sabbaths, who choose what pleases me and hold fast to my covenant—to them I will give within my temple and its walls a memorial and a name better than sons and daughters; I will give them an everlasting name that will endure forever.' —Isaiah 56:3-5

I got my first worship director job when I was going through a divorce while trying to reconcile my faith with my sexuality. Seems like a great time to start a new church gig, right? I felt unqualified to lead worship. I felt unworthy of a church home. Though the pastor who hired me understood my circumstances, I wasn't 100% sure that God and I were okay.

I was a Christian learning how to accept that I was gay.

I soon came to understand what a soft spot God has for outsiders. One example of this is in Isaiah 56, where God upends the status quo, essentially saying there are no foreigners and that a faithful eunuch is a celebrated child of God, not just a dry tree.

Eunuchs were differently-gendered and, according to Jewish law, unclean and unwelcome in the temple. They would fit under the LGBTQ+ umbrella for sure.

That's why I think there is some comfort in this passage for all of us, but especially those who experience themselves as inherently different. God's kingdom opens its arms to all of us, even though many churches would lead us to believe otherwise. We may feel unworthy, shameful, or built wrongly to accept God's invitation. But God assures us that we do, in fact, belong.

—BKS

How will you confront the shame that tells you that you're unworthy of God's acceptance and love?

WEDNESDAY OF THE THIRD WEEK OF LENT

The child grew and became strong, filled with wisdom; and the favor of God was upon him. —Luke 2:40

When I was a teenager, I formed a habit of spending two hours a day at the piano, working on scales, practicing pieces, and writing melodies. Those were hours I could've spent riding my bike or playing Atari games, and there were times I wanted to. But because I didn't, piano and songwriting became second nature to me.

A few years down the road, I began to understand music as my calling from God—something I might not have recognized and would not have been prepared for if I hadn't made music a daily practice. Teenage Me didn't know it, but I was soul training.

Jesus was a precocious twelve-year-old whose parents were good, observant Jews. Given what we know about Jesus as an adult, it's actually not too surprising that he would stay behind after Passover to sit with the temple teachers. Of course, Mary and Joseph were not happy about it when they discovered he wasn't with their caravan. When they found him, prepared to grab him by the collar and drag him back to Nazareth, he was perplexed, asking them, Didn't you know I'd be in my Father's house? He was soul training.

The rhythms and rituals of our youth don't just follow us into adulthood—they shape us as adults.

Soul training is the sum of those habits we form that help us recognize God and understand ourselves better.

Practicing piano can be a spiritual exercise. So can training for a marathon, photographing nature, or volunteering at an animal shelter. Jesus hanging out in the temple as a kid shaped him into the teacher he would become. He didn't come out of the womb with all this wisdom. He asked questions, listened closely, and became... well... Jesus.

—BKS

It's never too late to begin soul training. What interest or passion do you have that could serve as a spiritual exercise for you?

THURSDAY OF THE THIRD WEEK OF LENT

During the high priesthood of Annas and Caiaphas, the word of God came to John son of Zechariah in the wilderness.
—Luke 3:2

My history professor was short, fat, and unkempt, with an oily combover and a stained tie, who smoked during class. Dr. B's style, along with his harsh grading, made him unpopular among those scrambling for social status, but his course was required and I couldn't afford to be snobby.

By the end of that class I was hooked. Dr. B was always prepared, knew his stuff, and tied history to art and language, as well as redeemed any convoluted thought I babbled.

The last course I took from him probably saved my life.

At the end of my junior year I had decided to drop out. For months I had been repeatedly and publicly abused by a powerful faculty member. Exhausted, broken, and deeply ashamed, I couldn't imagine surviving another round. Showing up at Dr. B's office, I begged him to sign the paper that would set me free from my obligations if not my demons.

I don't remember what he said. But he turned me around, literally and academically, acting as light until I could see it myself.

I realize now that God had called him to his work and guided me to his care.

In Luke 3:1-3, Luke lists powerful rulers and then has John wander into the scene. John is the son of a priest of some stature, but a wild man who has been in the desert to fast and pray and learn, tilling the soil of his soul. When he hears God's word, John's *prepared*. God tells John to call people to repentance, a fancy way of saying to turn back toward God. John does.

While we don't know how many people John taught and saved through baptism, we know of at least one, Jesus, and that one is enough.

Not every weirdo is John the Baptizer and not every unkempt prof is Dr. B. To be the men they were, they had to prepare, listen when God spoke, and obey. That takes discipline of mind, body, and spirit, along with the ability to ignore the name-calling that comes when you aren't what others expect.

I don't know whether Dr. B ever got the respect he deserved, or how many people he rescued. But I know of at least one, and that one is enough for me.

—EOR

When has an unlikely rescuer shined light for you? What did that look like?

FRIDAY OF THE THIRD WEEK OF LENT

> Then Jesus was led up by the Spirit into the wilderness to be tempted by the devil. He fasted forty days and forty nights, and afterwards he was famished. —Matthew 4:1-2

We can't possibly be prepared for everything life throws at us, but we can prepare for some things. Like starting in January to save for a family vacation in June. Or studying (a lot) before you take the bar exam.

Sometimes we can brace ourselves for what we see coming—the declining health of our aging parents, the arrival of a new baby, or a job transfer to a new town. But even then, we cannot fully know how we'll be impacted, emotionally or otherwise.

Similarly, there are ways to prepare spiritually for things we are sure to face. Like Jesus did in the wilderness.

In Matthew 3, Jesus is baptized by John and then, is led by God's Spirit into the wilderness to prepare for what was ahead. Wildernesses are wild-nesses—pieces of our environment that can make us or break us. I've experienced a few in my years, and I usually find them without a map. But Jesus had an idea of what was coming and prepared himself by fasting.

As a spiritual practice, fasting is saying no to things like alcohol, social media, or Hulu, not because those things are inherently bad, but because saying no to them trains us to say no to other, more dangerous kinds of gratification.

Jesus was giving up food in order to have the spiritual stamina he would need when the tempter came, dangling shortcuts to glory in front of his face.

—BKS

What is something you've given up before in order to become stronger, faster, smarter, etc.?

What is something you'd be willing to fast from for a season to become more spiritually prepared for wisdom?

SATURDAY OF THE THIRD WEEK OF LENT

Then he went down with them and came to Nazareth, and was obedient to them. His mother treasured all these things in her heart. And Jesus increased in wisdom and in years, and in divine and human favor. —Luke 2:51-52

When my daughter was on the brink of womanhood I worried, even though she wasn't doing anything death-defying or dangerous. Unless by dangerous you mean working her mother's last nerve.

When they're toddlers, children expand their young egos with that annoying *No!* phase. My child postponed her *No!* phase for a decade while honing her skills in sarcasm.

So when pubescent Jesus misses the caravan home from Jerusalem, forcing his parents to return and track him down, my sympathies lie with his mother. Don't you know that Jesus rolled his eyes dramatically before snarking "Why were you searching for me? Did you not know that I must be in my Father's house?"

Brink-of-manhood Jesus has been in the temple arguing Torah with the men, expanding his ego. Scripture does not say that Mary, panicked and tired from searching for her missing child, backhanded the smart-mouthed savior, but I can imagine her wanting to.

She and Joseph lead Jesus back home to Nazareth where Jesus was obedient to them.

As Jesus grew, Mary must have depended on the God-given practices she had instilled: dedicating him to God as required (v. 39), observing Passover (v. 41), and, of course, the big "Let it be" she gave the angel when it told her she was pregnant.

The beginning and end of this passage link obedience with growth in wisdom (vs. 39-40, 51-52). When parents, whether divine or human, provide structure and expect obedience, they instill internal discipline. When children rebel, they grow in courage and experience. Obedience and rebellion, discipline and experience: these are the framework for wisdom.

God gave us the law to shape us for wisdom. We choose spiritual practices, such as obedience, to curb our adolescent No!s and strengthen our souls so that as we increase in years we, like Jesus, may also increase in divine and human favor.

—EOR

When adolescent urges toward rebellion control you, how might you use obedience to build self-discipline?

SUNDAY OF THE THIRD WEEK OF LENT

> And when he comes home, he calls together his friends and neighbors, saying to them, 'Rejoice with me, for I have found my sheep that was lost.' —Luke 15:6

On the Discipline of Celebration

When my son, Nick, was four years old, we lost him at a theme park. We were in one of those big souvenir shops right by the park's exit gate. Of course, we panicked. The staff at the store knew exactly what to do—I figure this wasn't their first preschooler rodeo.

They asked everyone to stop what they were doing and look for my son. In a matter of a couple minutes, he was back in my arms. Sure, I was upset that he'd gotten away from us. But I was so relieved he was safe, all I wanted to do was buy everyone in the store a funnel cake.

We've all lost things. Small things like car keys. Big things like a preschooler. Sometimes finding them is simply a relief. But sometimes, it's a reason to party.

Here, a shepherd finds a lost sheep, one of a hundred sheep, and he gathers his friends to celebrate. Later, a woman loses a coin—one of only ten she has to her name. When she finds it, she tells her friends and they rejoice together. And after that, a father, whose son has left home, throws a huge party when his wayward kid returns to him.

Celebrating the good things that happen, even small things, is a spiritual practice. Some of us minimize our successes, which can make drawing attention to them more challenging than, say, fasting. It's often easier to toast the good things that happen for others than it is to invite them to rejoice with us. But when we acknowledge and share our achievements, we give our friends an opportunity to show us love—something they like to do, and something that helps us see ourselves the way they do.

Whether for ourselves or someone else, keeping an eye out for a reason to celebrate, and then drawing attention to it with an attaboy, a cake, or a text to a friend that says "I did it!" is a way that we can make joy and gratitude something we experience on the regular. And couldn't we all use more of both?

—BKS

What is something you can celebrate today? Right now?

MONDAY OF THE THIRD WEEK OF LENT

Leave your gift there before the altar and go; first be reconciled to your brother or sister, and then come and offer your gift. —Matthew 5:24

On the Discipline of Reconciliation

Ever been on the receiving end of the silent treatment? You know, where someone isn't speaking to you, but you don't know why? I have. It can be funny to watch in a rom-com, but in real life, it's no fun.

Of course, what the injured party is (isn't) saying is you hurt my feelings, or you weren't listening the last twelve times I asked you not to do that. As the person who did the thing that hurt the other person, it is on me to go to them, take responsibility for what I did, and make things right.

We don't make altar sacrifices anymore, but what Jesus is saying here is: don't lay your lamb down at the altar if someone has something against you.

Sometimes I know what I did that wronged someone else. And sometimes it's a big deal. Making reconciliation in this context means owning what I did—or failed to do—and humbly asking forgiveness from the person I hurt. That is pretty impossible to do if I think I'm right, if I believe I'm owed something in return, or if I'm just downright stubborn. But until I lay down my pride, it will not only stand between me and the person I hurt, but also between me and God.

And that's the point. When my behavior has caused a rift with someone, and I don't do all I can to repair the relationship, then it causes a rift with God too. If I want to please God, then I have to be mindful of how I'm treating others.

—BKS

**Do you have a relationship that needs repairing?
What steps can you take to practice reconciliation?**

TUESDAY OF THE THIRD WEEK OF LENT

> I say to you that everyone who looks at another with lust has already committed adultery in his heart. —Matthew 5:28

<u>On the Discipline of Self-Control</u>

God created us as sensual beings who touch, taste, smell, see, hear, and experience. God also created beauty, beautifully, and made us sensitive to it. It is both fleshly and divine to experience the pull that beauty can have on us. It draws us nearer to God's own nature, to what God must feel when observing God's own creation.

That's not lust.

Lust is seeing an object or person, being drawn to it, and wanting to possess it. When we lust, a person is transformed in our minds into an object to be used or won. We lose sight of their dignity and self-determination. It's a tragedy, as the loss of holiness and humanity always is.

When I see a human being I find compelling and have a bodily reaction, that alone is not a problem. That's just how we're all made: stimulus then response. Lust happens when I take that response and let my imagination run wild. It isn't about sex, or even really about attraction, but about the rush I get. It's about the power and ego boost that comes from asserting myself and getting what I want.

But when I do that, I don't in any way take into consideration the well-being of the other person. In a split second, my mind can turn that human being—someone with their own desires, strengths, and history— into a kind of toy, or a tool, to be used to my own ends.

So how do we conquer lust? By dealing with our craving for power, as well as our feelings of powerlessness. By turning our thoughts toward the wholeness of the other person, seeing them as a subject, not an object.

Practices to counter lust include looking at people we find compelling and thinking through the fact that they are human beings too, with families, histories, struggles, etc. Or, when we are wrestling with our own powerlessness, we can learn to counter lust by affirming our power—reminding ourselves that we can and do make choices, and that we are not being deprived of our desires.

—EOR

Where is lust (the compulsion to conquer or possess another person) a problem for you?
How can you address it and deal with it?

WEDNESDAY OF THE FOURTH WEEK OF LENT

> He asked them, 'How many loaves do you have?' They said, 'Seven'....He took the seven loaves, and after giving thanks he broke them...and they distributed them to the crowd.
> —Mark 8:5-6

On the Discipline of Sacrifice

It had been a long day. The thousands who had gathered to hear Jesus teach were tired and hungry, and they still had to walk home. Jesus' disciples were hungry too. Between them, they had seven loaves of bread and a few small fish. When Jesus asked for their dinner, the disciples handed it over. There's no record of a scuffle, of words exchanged, or of any sore feelings. They just gave it to Jesus, not knowing what he was about to do with it.

Sacrifice is a concept we all understand. I've been on the receiving end of my parents' sacrifices, probably more than I realize. I've done without things so that my kids had what they wanted and needed. That's just a given. But I've never emptied my bank account to buy shoes for the homeless. I've never given one of my kidneys to a stranger who desperately needs one. I've never given my dinner to someone hungrier than me.

Sometimes God asks us to hand it over. And it's usually awkward, uncomfortable, even painful. We don't always know how our sacrifice will benefit someone else. We can't always trust its recipient. But because we trust God, we know that when we give it, God blesses it, and multiplies it.

Sacrifice as a spiritual practice can start small. Giving up lattes for a month and giving the money to a local homeless shelter to provide coffee for its guests might be a good starting point. Or delaying a weekend getaway and giving what you'd spend to support refugees who are starting a new life where you are.

—BKS

What is something valuable to you that are you willing to sacrifice to train your soul for good?

THURSDAY OF THE FOURTH WEEK OF LENT

> At daybreak he departed and went into a deserted place. And the crowds were looking for him; and when they reached him, they wanted to prevent him from leaving them. —Luke 4:42

On the Discipline of Solitude

Jesus had been dodging religious legalists, healing the sick, rebuking demons, and teaching constantly. I'm exhausted just thinking about it. We go and go and go and then we're surprised when we run out of gas. Why is that?

Our reserves of power are pretty small. AAA batteries at best. God's power is enormous. Jesus of Nazareth knew the limits of his body and spirit—how big his battery was. So to do all the things he did, he charged up with God's power, sneaking away at daybreak to be alone with God the Almighty.

We don't know exactly what he did while he was alone, but it's a good bet that he prayed, meditated, regrouped, and recharged. Jesus didn't spend time by himself with God in order to rest from his work. He drank in God's energy, God's power before he had to do what he did.

If you're a parent, or a caregiver, or a pastor, or just a person who cares about people who aren't you, let me remind you how vital solitude is. Those who tend to the needs of others face hazards—physical, emotional, and spiritual. We risk our souls sticking to the wrong things, such as unhealthy attention or adoration. We also risk having our spirits become blocked by cynicism, negativity, and just plain burnout.

Regularly setting aside time to drink from God's infinite power source is critical for refilling our spiritual batteries. Solitude is a discipline of gaining strength from God.

Time alone can be hard to get. We have to admit our need to anyone who depends on us and then ask for their support. Maybe all you can manage is a bath or some deep breathing while a little one is napping. Maybe you have more freedom and can negotiate an afternoon hike by yourself, take a long drive in the country, or even plan a solo weekend retreat.

But remember: For solitude to have its healing effect you must aim for minimal distractions and interactions, as well as plenty of space for quiet, prayer, reflection... and rest.

—BKS

How can you make solitude a regular part of your life?

FRIDAY OF THE FOURTH WEEK OF LENT

> But I say to you that listen, 'Love your enemies, do good to those who hate you, bless those who curse you, pray for those who abuse you.' —Luke 6:27-28

On the Discipline of Prayer

Throughout the Gospels, Jesus asks us to do some pretty crazy things. Among the craziest is expecting us to love our enemies. Of course, he knows it's more than we can do on our own because it's more than he could do on his own. But he showed us, all the way up to his last breath, that he could love those who hated him, and bless those who wanted him dead. And the crazy thing is, so can we.

We access God's power, courage, and well of love through prayer—consistent, expectant, soul-baring prayer. It gives us perspective when we're unsure, peace when we're anxious, and stamina when ours is gone. Turns out the result of this kind of prayer is often grace: the ability to do what we could not otherwise do.

Loving one's enemies is never easy. In fact, I'd argue it can't be done without God's help. When someone has hurt us deeply, wanting their good is truly hard. But in those cases, we can plead with God to do what we can't.

If prayer is difficult for you, you might begin by reading the prayers of others, as in *The Book Of Common Prayer* or any of the countless collections available. You might also try writing out your prayers in a journal, or picking a time each day to go to God.

Loving those who've hurt us or who wish us ill is among the hardest things we do. Let God do the heavy lifting.

—BKS

**Who is your enemy?
How can you pray for them today?**

SATURDAY OF THE FOURTH WEEK OF LENT

They went to him and woke him up, shouting, 'Master, Master, we are perishing!' — Luke 8:24a

<u>On the Discipline of Rest</u>

Jesus was tired and looking for a respite from the crowds, so he got into a boat with his disciples and set out to cross the Sea of Galilee. After a bit, Jesus fell asleep and while he was sleeping, a storm came up suddenly. The boat began to fill with water and the disciples—who, by the way, were experienced fishermen and had no doubt encountered rough water before—woke Jesus in a panic, probably because he was sleeping through the tumult. He rebuked the wild wind and waves and everything was calm again.

Then Jesus asked them, "Where is your faith?" (v. 25)

In the middle of the storm the disciples feared for their safety, didn't trust their own abilities to keep the boat from sinking, and didn't lean on the faith they professed. Conversely, Jesus could rest because he trusted everyone—including God—would be okay and that they could manage the world without him for a bit.

Rest requires trust. If I'm worried about paying my mortgage, saving my marriage, or keeping my career afloat, I won't rest. I'll keep doing everything I do to right the ship, so to speak. But if I trust that everything in my world is in capable hands and that all will be well, I can let go of the wheel and rest.

To practice rest I might delegate a responsibility and let go of the outcome, so that the video game I play to relax is actually restful. The point of rest is not just about taking a break, but also giving up control and trusting that everything will be fine while you do.

—BKS

What are some actions you can practice to deepen your trust in God and others so that you can experience rest?

SUNDAY OF THE FOURTH WEEK OF LENT

> Now as they went on their way, he entered a certain village, where a woman named Martha welcomed him into her home. — Luke 10:38

<u>On the Discipline of Fellowship</u>

Jesus brought all his disciples to Mary and Martha's house for dinner. Mary hung out with the disciples and listened to Jesus tell stories while Martha stressed out over getting their meal together. When Martha finally lost her cool, Jesus assured her that Mary had done nothing wrong, even implying that Martha could join them too.

The fact is these kinds of gatherings were the heartbeat of family life in Jesus' day. The kind of fellowship small groups in churches aspire to have. It was in community that children were raised, physical needs were met, and souls were filled. In John 21, resurrected Jesus cooked fish and invited his disciples. Of all the things Jesus could've chosen to do, fellowship was right at the top of his list.

When my grandmother died, friends from her tiny, tightly knit community brought countless casseroles, covered dishes, Jello salads, and sweets when they stopped by to offer their condolences to our family. The stories, laughter, and tears were a balm for my grandfather's broken heart. In times like those, where there is inexpressible pain and grief, love can be expressed and felt through fried chicken and fellowship.

Because of the pandemic, most of us have felt isolated to some degree. Depression, addiction, and anxiety are at troubling levels. What if the remedy for this isolation is reaching out with kindness, hope, and love, and allowing ourselves to receive the same?

It's true that sometimes what we want and need is time and space to process and mourn. And sometimes, fellowship is how God chooses to remind us that, in the midst of everything, we are not alone.

—BKS

**How do you allow fellowship into your life?
How might you practice it with others?**

MONDAY OF THE FOURTH WEEK OF LENT

In the morning, while it was still very dark, he got up and went out to a deserted place, and there he prayed. —Mark 1:35

<u>On the Disciplines of Solitude and Prayer</u>

Once again, Jesus sneaks off by himself to pray. How else was he going to get a little peace and quiet? With his notoriety growing, people were always chasing him with their questions, their afflictions, and their accusations. Claiming solitary time with his Father was getting harder and harder to do.

For Jesus, prayer was preparation.

When Simon finds him, he has been praying about the corner he knows his ministry is about to turn. He is confident when he says, "Let's go do what I came out to do."

Connecting with God refilled his spirit, renewed his strength, and steadied his resolve.

Solitude makes room for uninterrupted, spirit-filling, soul-focusing prayer. That prayer gives us what we need to face what we see coming, and what we don't.

Like Jesus, we all lead crowded, noisy lives, with people who count on us. But when he knew he needed time with God, Jesus was fine with stepping away from everything and everyone to get alone and pray.

Am I fine with stepping away? My sense of duty, and my guilt over maybe letting someone down, has held me in place many, many times. I am learning that most things can actually wait. But when the thing I need is prayer, I will only recognize it if prayer is a practice.

—BKS

Where do you find solitude?
How can you make solitary prayer a spiritual practice?

TUESDAY OF THE FOURTH WEEK OF LENT

God is spirit, and those who worship him must worship in spirit and truth. —John 4:24

On the Discipline of Worship

Leading people in the worship of God is something that I do. I can create a worshipful environment. I can orchestrate activities like music, prayer, and silence. I can give people words to say, sing, and even pray. But if those with me aren't actually worshiping, then they might as well be at a Benton Stokes concert.

When we worship God, we express the beauty, goodness, grace, and power of God. That's what liturgical activities like singing and prayer are for. They focus our attention on the awesome attributes of God, allowing us to see God more clearly, and gain the vital perspective that gives.

Jesus distinguishes worship as a practice from worship as an internal experience. The spiritual exercise of worship always involves words, phrases, and behaviors we value, even when we are worshiping alone. The experience of worship results in awe, peace, gratitude, joy, and more. We need both. And the ways we go about it are as diverse as we are.

Worship as a discipline is an act of will or habit. Worship as an experience is an act of mind and body.

When we worship in spirit and truth, we join our spirits with the Holy Spirit, and we ascribe to God what we know to be true. Giving God praise and adoration, and doing so with mind, body, soul, spirit, and will, is the kind of worship God enjoys.

—BKS

When do you feel most engaged in worshiping God? Why do you think worship is sometimes hard for you?

WEDNESDAY OF THE FIFTH WEEK OF LENT

> Now about eight days after these sayings Jesus took with him Peter and John and James and went up on the mountain to pray.
> —Luke 9:28

On the Discipline of Transparency

When I was first coming out, I didn't call up everyone in my contacts and say, "Hey, I'm gay." There are a few, hopefully obvious, reasons why. But mostly, I was only willing to come out to those I thought would love and accept me after the big conversation.

Turns out I was lucky. And so was Jesus.

He didn't share his coming out with everyone either. Peter, James, and John had proven themselves to be faithful disciples. Yes, there was a risk they'd sell their story to the tabloids. Or maybe run for the hills, never to be seen again. It was not a given that Jesus' reveal would go the way he hoped. But he wanted to share this thing about himself with his close friends, so he took the chance and chose to be transparent.

Allowing ourselves to be seen always comes with risks. Rejection hurts. But when we hide, we settle for a version of ourselves that is less brilliant than we were meant to be. We deprive the world of our glory.

For Jesus, his glory was his divine nature. Because we were all created in God's image, we each have some God-ness inside us, a spark that is fanned into glory as we nurture and share it.

As I've become more and more open about all kinds of things in recent years, I've allowed more of my own glory to show. And God uses that in ways I'll never even know.

—BKS

Who are you willing to show your glory to?
How can you share your glory with the world?

THURSDAY OF THE FIFTH WEEK OF LENT

> And Jesus said, 'Neither do I condemn you. Go your way, and from now on do not sin again.' —John 8:11b

On the Discipline of Forgiveness

The Pharisees had Jesus in a conundrum for sure. What they were about to do was completely within the realm of the law.

Adulterers were stoned. Yes, it was barbaric, but it was the understood punishment for the crime—and adultery was a crime. Was Jesus going to contradict the law of Moses in front of them, God, and everybody?

Jesus knelt down and started writing in the dirt. It's unclear what he wrote, but his scribblings figured into the men's reactions as he offered a proposition: If any of you is sinless, go ahead and hit her with a stone (v. 7) They all dropped their rocks, one by one, and went home.

Forgiveness is releasing one's right to revenge or repayment. Because of the law of their society, it was within the rights of the Pharisees to stone the woman. They relinquished that right, and in doing so, forgave her. Jesus himself forgave her as well when he said to her, "I don't condemn you either. Go and sin no more."

Forgiveness is a big thing to ask and a big thing to give. I know what it means to lay down my stone, and it isn't easy. I've also been the offender who received forgiveness. Both brought me peace and freedom. Forgiveness is powerful like that.

—BKS

When have you chosen to forgive someone?
When have you received forgiveness you knew you didn't deserve?

FRIDAY OF THE FIFTH WEEK OF LENT

> Mary took a pound of costly perfume made of pure nard,
> anointed Jesus' feet, and wiped them with her hair.
> —John 12:7

On the Discipline of Accepting Care & Love

Suppose you are a person who gives. A lot. You give your time, your resources, your attention, your care. You give to your friends, of course, but also to strangers you don't even know. People in need seem to find you, and you help them. You're that person.

Now suppose someone who loves you empties their savings account to send you on a spa vacation to Bali. She does this because 1) she thinks you deserve it, 2) she wants to share her gratitude with you for what you've done for her, and 3) she knows you need care, but won't do it for yourself. She's been paying attention, like a good friend does.

Now, you have this frenemy who finds out about the gift and points out that if HIS friend was going to spend HER savings, she could help a lot of people. And he would be happy to oversee the dispersing of generosity.

You could respond to your frenemy from a place of guilt or shame saying, "You know, you're right. Others need care more than I do"' and return the gift. Many of us would. But instead, you take to heart what your friend gave you, acknowledge the magnitude of the gift—and the love behind it—and get on that plane for Bali.

When we accept care from someone, especially when we actually need it, it isn't a selfish act. Instead it grows our compassion for others, especially for the giver.

—BKS

When have you accepted care from someone who loves you? Who do you love who really needs your offer of care today...whether they accept it or not?

SATURDAY OF THE FIFTH WEEK OF LENT

He went to Nazareth, where he had been brought up, and on the Sabbath day he went into the synagogue, as was his custom. He stood up to read... —Luke 4:16

On the Disciplines of Study & Sabbath-Keeping

Jesus, the rebel.

Jesus, the table-turner, the prophet, the counter-cultural feminist lover of outcasts.

Do you know that Jesus?

Me too. I like that Jesus. He's totally rock-n-roll.

But this passage makes me look at another Jesus, who probably never even owned a motorcycle jacket like the one in my closet.

The Jesus in Luke 4:16 is a study-er, a sabbath-keeper, a traditional traveling rabbi, a respecter of the law and of tradition. Even as an adult he does what he is supposed to do, which is what his parents did, which is what their parents did.

Imagine Jesus having to fill out one of those little biographical boxes on job applications. Or completing his social media profile. Prophet. Rabble-rouser. Son of Man, and of Joseph, son of Jacob of the line of David.

Every time you think of Jesus breaking boundaries and naming hypocrisy, think also of the Jesus of Luke 4:16.

Jesus, still connected to his childhood home, goes to visit. And while he's there he heads over to the local adult education center—the synagogue—on the Sabbath, because that is what he is in the habit of doing.

Jesus is in the habit of study, in the habit of keeping the Sabbath, in the habit of honoring his ancestry.

The real Jesus was formed by a lifetime of spiritually strengthening habits—study, Sabbath, honoring family, and others—into a man who could also be a rebel, a prophet, a rescuer and healer.

That is the power of spiritual practice that becomes habit: it shapes our souls and our selves into wall-crushers, derision-riskers, humble servants of God and others.

My Jesus spent his life preparing to welcome rebellious sinners like me into his Father's house. Seems like he might have gotten that whole lifestyle thing right.

—EOR

What spiritual preparation(s) are you making a regular part of your life?

SUNDAY OF THE FIFTH WEEK OF LENT

> On the third day there was a wedding in Cana of Galilee, and the mother of Jesus was there. —John 2:1

On the Discipline of Celebration

Jesus loved a party. In the Gospels, there are many accounts of Jesus hanging out with friends, feasting, laughing, telling stories. It's not surprising that his first miracle happened at a wedding. Celebration is a big part of life with God.

I grew up with the notion that Jesus was a pretty serious guy. And that God was a cranky, old deity. Many of the depictions of Jesus show him looking wistful, pained, or melancholy. Sure, he had those moments, as we all do. I think Jesus had a lighter side too. People wouldn't have been so drawn to him if he were always a wet sweater.

As for us, there are plenty of times when we don't feel like celebrating. Life is full of disappointment, trips to the DMV and the dentist, and legit reasons to be downtrodden. But those times are made easier when I picture a joyful God, dancing to Motown, laughing at a funny story, and celebrating life's big and small milestones with us.

Jesus didn't have to turn water into wine. He wanted to, maybe because he loved a party. Just like his Father.

—BKS

What is one thing in your life (or in the larger world) that is worthy of celebrating?

What are three activities you can take to celebrate today?

MONDAY OF THE FIFTH WEEK OF LENT

> Now during those days he went out to the mountain to pray; and he spent the night in prayer to God. And when day came, he called his disciples and chose twelve of them, whom he also named apostles. —Luke 6:12-13

<u>*On the Disciplines of Solitude & Prayer*</u>

I don't always trust myself. When it comes to making decisions of any magnitude, I can end up paralyzed, afraid of making the wrong choice. Maybe you've been there. I've sometimes delayed and deferred until the choice just never gets made, at least not by me.

Jesus was at one of those important crossroads. He needed to choose the twelve men who would continue his work after he was gone. Because he'd made a habit of pulling away from the crowds and his friends to pray, he could hear and recognize his Father's voice when he needed discernment. After spending the night in prayer, Jesus was able to name his apostles.

Discernment is divine insight, perceptiveness that doesn't come from research, option-weighing, or gut instinct. When I get stuck on a decision, I ask God for discernment. But here's the thing: if I haven't made a habit of spending time alone with God in prayer, how am I going to recognize God's voice if discernment is offered to me?

Jesus knew God's voice, and so can we. But it requires consistently talking to and listening for God in quiet, solitary moments. It takes practice.

—BKS

What is a decision you're making that could benefit from discernment?
How will you know God's voice if you hear it?

TUESDAY OF THE FIFTH WEEK OF LENT

> Then Jesus told his disciples, 'If any want to become my followers, let them deny themselves and take up their cross and follow me. For those who want to save their life will lose it, and those who lose their life for my sake will find it. For what will it profit them if they gain the whole world but forfeit their life? Or what will they give in return for their life?'
> —Matthew 16:24-26

On the Discipline of Ego-Denial

Jesus had an ego. All humans do. The tempter knew this when he approached Jesus in the desert. The temptations Jesus faced—to feed everyone, to rule the world, to prove he was the Son of God—all fed his ego. Saying no to them took real fortitude. But because he had practiced denying himself by fasting, by not having to have the last word, by living in humility, he was able to withstand the temptations and say no to his own ego.

When we deny ourselves, we trade our ideas of what we deserve, or what we think should be, for what is in line with the Spirit.

Like a doctor who quits her successful practice to treat patients in a third-world country, because that's what she feels led to do. Or an ordinary guy who donates his tax refund to feed homeless folks instead of spending a weekend with his friends in Tahoe.

It's hard saying no to my ego because my self-image is wrapped up in what I've achieved, what I possess, and how I present myself to the world. But denying myself gets me unstuck from a specific idea of who I am, or what I deserve. It frees me up to serve God in ways I didn't even know were possible. And my spirit grows stronger as it is becomes more closely aligned with God's Spirit.

—BKS

What is something you could deny yourself in order to grow closer to God?

WEDNESDAY OF THE SIXTH WEEK OF LENT

It will not be so among you; whoever wishes to be great among you must be your servant, and whoever wishes to be first among you must be your slave —Matthew 20:26-27

<u>On the Disciplines of Ego-Denial & Service</u>

I started out at Starbucks as a part-time barista. Before long, I realized I really liked working there. I was promoted to store manager in about six months. I enjoyed making lattes, chatting up customers, doing dishes, and taking out trash alongside my baristas. I'd often take on the task nobody loved doing to remind myself what it means to serve.

Jesus was the consummate servant-leader. He found joy in taking care of the needs of others. He didn't expect the disciples to do anything he didn't do himself. He also didn't expect to be called King.

Great leaders don't name themselves leaders and then demand people to follow. They lead by example, serving everyone with respect, and putting themselves last.

Service requires self-denial. I can't serve others well if I'm telling myself I deserve better. I learn to say no to my ego by doing without, by not having to have the last word, and by choosing to be last in line.

—BKS

What are some qualities you've seen in servant-leaders you admire? What one step can you take to cultivate those qualities within yourself?

THURSDAY OF THE SIXTH WEEK OF LENT

He was praying in a certain place, and after he had finished, one of his disciples said to him, 'Lord, teach us to pray, as John taught his disciples.' —Luke 11:1

On the Discipline of Prayer

Those of us who pray in public—pastors, teachers, rabbis, worship leaders— are prone to a number of annoying habits.

Any of these sound familiar?

Some pray-ers call God by special names that can be confusing and exclusionary.

Some use flowery language, or big vocabulary words that do more to draw attention to the pray-er than to God.

Some sound like auctioneers, while others sound like they're on C-SPAN.

Some end every clause with "Father" or "Lord" as if everyone (God included) needs to be reminded who's being addressed.

Not to criticize anyone's intentions, but the bottom line is this: we overcomplicate our prayers.

Whether praying in public or alone with God, it serves us well to remember the prayer that Jesus taught his disciples. When we pray the way Jesus did, we simply acknowledge that God is giving and forgiving, powerful and wise, and so much bigger than we are.

Jesus' prayer is offered humbly, giving God reverence and worship. It is not me-focused, but us-focused, expressing the bodily needs and soul needs of everyone. It is simple and sincere, without fancy or frivolous language.

It is surprising what we learn about ourselves and about God when we pray like Jesus did.

—BKS

A practice to try on
Pray the Lord's Prayer, pausing after each phrase to reflect on its meaning to you in that moment.

FRIDAY OF THE SIXTH WEEK OF LENT

> He went to him and bandaged his wounds, having poured oil and wine on them. Then he put him on his own animal, brought him to an inn, and took care of him. —Luke 10:34

On the Discipline of Service

What does it mean to love my neighbor?

If I define love as willing the good of another person, then I guess I could start by not bringing them harm. COVID-19 has given me opportunities to love my neighbor every time I leave my home. And heck: wearing a mask is easy.

Beyond that, loving my neighbor can get messy. It starts with paying attention to the needs of others around me. Obviously, if someone is lying on the side of the road, injured and afraid, I'm probably going to notice. But then I have to choose whether, and how, to get involved.

Samaritans weren't very liked by Jews. They differed over many things, including the chosen place to worship God. So when Jesus makes a Samaritan the protagonist of his morality tale, those in audience where aghast.

Good men—priests, scholars, leaders—pass by their nearly-dead neighbor. The bad Samaritan tends to the traveler's wounds, puts him on his animal, takes him to an inn, and pays for his room, promising to return the next day to check on him. Turns out anyone can love well.

Love is often expressed in service. Giving a neighbor a ride to the doctor, buying a meal for someone who's hungry, or doing simple home repairs for an elderly person are all ways we love each other. Loving my neighbor simply starts with asking myself, "How can I help?"

—BKS

What is one action you can repeatedly take to train yourself to better notice the true needs of those around you?

SATURDAY OF THE SIXTH WEEK OF LENT

> This took place to fulfill what had been spoken through the prophet...The disciples went and did as Jesus had directed them. —Matthew 21:4, 6

On the Discipline of Submission

It feels good to be celebrated. Now, while we've established that Jesus was maybe the least egotistical guy that ever lived, he did, in fact, have an ego.

If I were Jesus, a ride through Jerusalem while people chanted "Hosanna! Blessed is he who comes in the name of the Lord!" would've felt at least a little gratifying. I mean, consider everything he'd denied himself up till now. Finally his work was being lifted up.

But honestly, I think Jesus would've been fine forgoing the parade if it would've made the dark days to follow any easier. Entering Jerusalem unannounced meant riding past the rebels the Romans were crucifying. Jesus had to know this might not go well for him. But he had chosen to do it, and saw it through, because of love.

Jesus was willing the good of everyone there—and a l of us—as he accepted the hosannas and arrived at what was to come.

I'll be honest: I don't like to submit. I respect authority, but I like for it to be my idea. Submission, even to God, often feels like it bumps into my kingdom...because it does.

There are things over which I have a modicum of control that I prefer not to hand over. In this passage Jesus was handing over all the control he had, or felt like he had, to God's will.

I'm not convinced he knew exactly what was about to happen, he knew—as do we—that doing what God asks is the good and right thing to do.

Submission was about to become the central theme of Jesus' remaining days.

—BKS

How can you make submission a central theme for your life in the coming days?

SUNDAY OF THE SIXTH WEEK OF LENT

At that same hour Jesus rejoiced in the Holy Spirit and said, 'I thank you, Father, Lord of heaven and earth, because you have hidden these things from the wise and the intelligent and have revealed them to infants; yes, Father, for such was your gracious will.' —Luke 10:21

<u>On the Discipline of Celebration in the Midst of Mystery</u>

God loves to use foolish things to confound the wise, to humble the intelligent, to exalt the simple, or just to remain impossible to figure out. Whyever that is, I'm confident that God's ways are both perfect and higher than mine.

I love that Jesus found such joy in the absurdity of his Father's mysterious ways. The Holy Spirit was rejoicing too—maybe the Trinity was just having a big cosmic laugh. At any rate, Jesus understood, better than anyone, that God doesn't work the way we do.

In God's upside-down kingdom, the weak are strong, the poor are rich, and the uneducated are wise. Babies are in on it too. The whole thing is bonkers!

Jesus took a moment to really revel in what was happening. In retrospect, I sometimes see what God has done in my life and I smile, or even laugh, at how the right pieces fell into place. But I rarely catch it in the moment. Jesus saw it, stopped what he was doing, and thanked God right then and there.

I want to enjoy what God is doing in my world. That begins with noticing God at work. I get there by shifting my focus from myself through practices like fasting, and giving my attention to God through solitude and prayer. Then as I pay attention, I celebrate what God is doing—also a spiritual practice.

—BKS

When was the last time you experienced joy by noticing what God was doing in your life?

Right now, take a moment to notice and to celebrate.

MONDAY OF THE SIXTH WEEK OF LENT

He answered, 'I tell you, if these were silent, the stones would shout out.' —Luke 19:40

<u>On the Discipline of Worship</u>

I've always been fascinated with studies of nature-versus-nurture. You know, where kids—often twins or adopted children—are studied during childhood and adolescence to see which of their traits can be attributed to genetics, and which are shaped by environment.

I'm a middle-aged guy, and I'm still noticing things that I do that are just like my mom or my dad. It's weird.

I love Jesus' comeback to the cranky Pharisees who want him to tell his people to stop their praising. He says, If they shut up, the stones will start shouting. That's because the worship of God exists in the DNA of everything.

We all come pre-loaded with the desire to worship God. It's in our nature.

As we grow, our environment influences whether we choose to worship God or to worship someone or something else. That's the nurture part. There are countless attention-grabbers competing for my adoration. I won't list them all, but heck, my own ego is in there swinging.

Because God gives me the freedom to decide who or what I worship, I don't always choose well. So worshiping God is a spiritual practice that focuses on engaging my whole self in the praise and adoration of my Creator, and nothing and no one else.

—BKS

What competes with God to be the object of your worship? Why do you think that is?

TUESDAY OF THE SIXTH WEEK OF LENT

If we live by the Spirit, let us also be guided by the Spirit.
—Galatians 5:25

There are six parts to each of us: mind, body, will, environment, spirit, and soul. Nobody has a livable, physical life if they're missing any one of them. Also—and this is important—none of our parts is inherently evil.

Mind, body, will, and environment are pretty easy concepts to grasp, but spirit and soul are a bit more ephemeral.

My spirit is my divine spark, created in God's image. It connects me to God, kinda like a cosmic USB cable of infinite length. Everyone's spirit is unique, sacred, and beautiful. When my spirit vibes with God's Spirit, I feel at peace. When it doesn't, I don't. That's when I'm more likely to mistrust myself, and doubt God's care for me.

So what can cause my spirit to get out-of-sync with God's? Lots of things, but most often, I look at what's going on with my soul.

Our souls stick to things. They aren't ever really satisfied by anything but God, but certainly will attach to other things if we let them. To keep my sticky soul from doing that, I have to be intentional about what I feed my mind, how I treat my body, and how I allow myself to be affected by my environment.

For example, if I choose to cyberstalk my ex, while eating a box of Little Debbie's, with Jerry Springer on the tv, then I'm giving my soul lots of unhealthiness to grab onto.

Over time, any one of those things could have repercussions for my soul. And none of those things would ever satisfy it, causing me to consume more and more, while feeling increasingly empty.

Getting to a place of soul-satisfaction and true spirit-peace requires us to choose things like kindness, patience, and self-control (*see verses 22-23*). Spiritual disciplines, like fasting and prayer, help us get in the practice of being more self-sacrificial and loving.

—BKS

What is something your soul likes to stick to?
How do you know when your spirit is out-of-sync with God's Spirit?

Holy Week

WEDNESDAY OF HOLY WEEK

Then he poured water into a basin and began to wash the disciples' feet and to wipe them with the towel that was tied around him. -John 13:5

<u>On the Discipline of Service</u>

So Elton John—whom I admire a great deal as a musician, a songwriter, and a human—came to my house in San Jose and made me dinner. He also did my laundry, and cleaned up my bathroom, which was a mess. After he folded my socks and loaded the dishwasher, he signed my favorite Elton album, and was on his way.

Okay, that didn't happen. (Did I have you going??) But if it had, it would've been almost as weird as this:

Jesus and his disciples had just finished their Passover meal. Jesus stood up, took off his tunic, and tied a towel around his waist. He poured water into a basin, and then made it really awkward for the disciples—he went around the room, washing their dirty, sandal-funky feet.

There are a few remarkable things about this. In their culture, feet were washed only by the lowest servant in a household—it was like the dirtiest, most undignified job you can think of.

Also, a teacher could not demean one of his students by asking them to wash his feet, so the idea that a teacher would wash a student's feet was unthinkable. I mean, can you imagine someone you idolize kneeling down and washing your feet? Or doing your laundry? Or cleaning your house? I can't.

One more thing: the disciples often bickered about which of them was most deserving of Jesus' favor. None of them would have offered to wash everyone's feet. But by humbling himself this way, Jesus is again demonstrating the last-shall-be-first nature of his Father's kingdom.

No one is great just because they say they are. The last becomes first by choosing to be last.

Serving others is messy. It can be thankless and humiliating. It also helps us become more like our Servant-savior Jesus.

—BKS

When have you served someone else, really truly expecting nothing (including gratitude) in return?
How can you make service a regular practice in your life?

MAUNDY THURSDAY

> He said, 'Abba, Father, for you all things are possible; remove this cup from me; yet, not what I want, but what you want.'
> —Mark 14:36

<u>On the Disciplines of Transparency, Prayer, & Submission</u>

You've been to Gethsemane. Not the garden, but the point of crisis it is known for. You have faced a reality—a diagnosis, a relationship impasse, a reckoning of some sort. This new reality brought difficult choices, emotionally-charged actions and reactions, and outcomes both surprising and predictable.

You probably prayed. You might've tried to bargain with God. I did both.

I can tell you that if I'd been Jesus, facing the cross, I'd have been looking around Gethsemane for an exit that didn't involve running into Judas and some burly Roman soldiers. Jesus didn't do that. But he also didn't start down that awful road without first asking God, "Could this be accomplished some other way?"

When I came to my Gethsemane, I wasn't staring down my own death, but the death of my marriage. It had followed years of self-discovery, excruciatingly honest conversations with my wife, and many painstaking steps toward self-acceptance. I'd begged with God repeatedly for another way, but I knew being honest about my sexuality meant breaking up my marriage. It was the only way we'd both find healing and peace.

Though I knew God would be with me, I really didn't know how it would turn out.

Even if Jesus knew what would happen after—I'm not convinced he did—he couldn't see all the awful that was coming, even if he had an inkling. Still he trusted God, and after he pleaded for a reprieve, he made a vow of surrender. Not what I want, but what you want.

—BKS

What's your Gethsemane? How did—or will—you face it?

GOOD FRIDAY

> Then Jesus said, 'Father, forgive them; for they do not know what they are doing.' —Luke 23:34

<u>On the Discipline of Prayer</u>

I have a hard time asking God to forgive some people.

Anti-maskers, anti-vaxxers, right-wing rioters, and voting-rights thieves: all hard. I *want* God to rain locusts down on rich people who say they pay too much in taxes, and to raise an unsightly rash on those who think people of color, queer folks, and immigrants have too much power already. (I don't pray for these things, but I want to, sometimes.)

Growing up in the South I heard older ladies cluck, "They don't know any better" when people behaved in small-minded ways. I don't believe ignorance is the culprit, but it does cause me to pause and pray: for myself, to love them, and for them, that God would change their hearts.

On the day Jesus died, no one knew exactly what they were doing when they betrayed, denied, and crucified him. Sure, the Romans knew they were squashing a likely uprising. And the Pharisees were surely ridding themselves of a challenge. His accusers, both the powerful and the rabble, had clear, compelling reasons.

But they didn't know they were murdering the One who would always love them.

As he was dying, Jesus prayed, "Father, forgive them, for they do not know what they are doing." He was praying for the Romans and the Pharisees, and Judas and Peter, and you and me. He knew that when we are hard-hearted, or frightened, or arrogant, we do awful things without realizing just how horrible they are.

Unlike me, Jesus had no trouble asking God to forgive. He had spent his whole life practicing prayer-filled love.

—BKS

**Who can you pray God's forgiveness for, today?
What has kept you from praying for them before?**

HOLY SATURDAY

On the sabbath they rested according to the commandment. — Luke 23:56b

On the Discipline of Waiting

Imagine that someone you love very much, to whom you have devoted your days and nights and heart and mind, dies and you are not allowed to be near them.

You aren't allowed to say goodbye because you would be infected by them, forcing you to isolate for days.

Because you would be unsafe, and you would bring danger to everyone around you.

Because it is against the law, and you believe in the rule of law.

It used to be tough to understand the situation the women disciples were in. Almost impossible to imagine not racing to the most important person in your life.

It's not so hard to imagine now, years into COVID, is it?

The execution of rebel leaders and crowd favorites could inspire riots in Jerusalem. Killing Jesus on a Friday afternoon assured the rulers of a certain level of managed pain: Friday evenings and Saturdays were the Sabbath, when those who loved God and did what God mandated stayed near home.

Jesus had loved God and had done what God had commanded. So had his followers. Everyone knew that when they crucified a rebel leader, his followers would be next to die. The rulers of Jerusalem could count on Jesus' followers scattering.

And, for the Jews, though washing and tending a dead loved one was a sacred act, it also infected you ritually, made you unable to attend temple or be around others.

At this point it's all not so hard to imagine, is it?

And so the women who loved Jesus waited for Sunday's dawn. They waited through the dark horror of the Sabbath evening, through Saturday's sorrowful celebrations, and through the next dangerous night. They waited for Sunday to finally say goodbye.

Waiting is so hard. Torturous even. Waiting is also a spiritual practice that trains us to live in the current moment while anticipating the next.

—EOR

**How are you training for this moment?
What are you choosing to not act on for the sake of what is to come?**

Easter

EASTER SUNDAY

> Jesus said to her, 'Mary!' She turned and said to him in Hebrew,' Rabbouni!' (which means Teacher). —John 20:16

If I had busted out of a tomb like El Chapo did from Puento Grande prison, I'd saunter into my favorite watering hole, order up a seltzer, and casually say to the shocked server, "Yeah, man, just got tired of death."

Not Jesus. Jesus trusted his truth with a tiny and peculiar group. He took three of his apprentices up a mountain to see his coming out as savior of Israel as long-gone Moses and Elijah showed up in a literal blaze of glory.

Then he told them to not tell anyone what they saw.

Later, on the third day after his death, Mary was at Jesus' tomb, terrified that his body had been taken. In her weeping she mistook him for the gardener when he walked up. But when he said her name, she recognized the sound and responded without hesitation, "Teacher'!

Mary could have told anyone she wanted that she'd seen him. But she wouldn't have been believed. So when Jesus appears, it's no stunt reveal, no subversive proclamation to a gossip. It's her friend showing up, revealing his own hidden truth, to reassure her and give her hope.

Unlike me and El Chapo, Jesus didn't want people to be impressed by his miraculous feat. He wanted to share the most important parts of himself one by one with people he could trust.

Jesus didn't aim to impress with wildly improbable events. It's just that that death couldn't keep him from showing up for a friend.

Jesus wants us to know him so intimately that we know the sound of his voice when he speaks our names. Even if people don't believe us when we say that he conquered death, or think we're nuts when we say we trust him, he'd rather show us his real self, his deeply loving self, than have us go gaga over some pyrotechnic show.

Jesus escaped from a physical tomb. Our tombs tend to be things like self-doubt, envy, anger, loss, and grief.

Jesus would rather we escape from our own tombs than be overly impressed by what he did with his.

—BKS & EOR

When have you recognized Jesus' voice?
What tombs have you yet to leave?

EASTER MONDAY (EASTER 2)

> When he was at the table with them, he took bread, blessed and broke it, and gave it to them. Then their eyes were opened, and they recognized him; and he vanished from their sight. — Luke 24:30-31

On the Discipline of Eucharist

Kids absorb the ideas adults repeat to them.

Getting dressed for my childhood church meant using bobby pins to secure a little lace handkerchief on my head because it's respectful. To this day I feel just a little naked going bareheaded during Worship.

I also knew that when taking Holy Communion you must never bite down on the host (the flat wafer used in some ancient-tradition churches) because you'll be biting Jesus.

The mental picture of me biting Jesus still haunts me. When I take Communion in a church that uses hosts I wait for that little dry bread to dissolve in my mouth, however long it takes, while everyone around me is chomping on Christ's body.

That ritual dining event we call *Communion* or *Eucharist* matters, and not only because the Apostle Paul spent a good chunk of I Corinthians talking about it. When you take Communion as a spiritual practice, Jesus shows up.

Two disciples are walking to Emmaus on Resurrection Day. Jesus starts walking with them. They don't recognize him, even though they walk together for hours while Jesus lectures them on the scriptural and historical relevance of his death and detombment.

They get where they're going and invite this chatty stranger in. Only at the table, when he breaks the bread, do they recognize him. It is in the breaking of the bread that they really see Jesus.

Jesus was with them the whole day, but when they remembered him with bread, he showed up in a wholly different way.

I suspect those two disciples, those spiritual kids, remembered everything about Communion after Jesus repeated it with them.

—EOR

**How might you incorporate Holy Communion into your worship practices, even when your church doesn't?
How can you make room for Jesus to show up?**

TUESDAY—EASTER 3

Jesus said to them, 'Come and have breakfast.' Now none of the disciples dared to ask him, 'Who are you?' because they knew it was the Lord. —John 21:12

On the Discipline of Fellowship

I love breakfast. I love when a friend shows up unexpectedly and says, Let's have breakfast. I've never had a friend come back from the dead and invite me to breakfast but that would be nice too, I suppose.

Jesus had to know his disciples were feeling lost without him. Like we feel when we can't hug those closest to us. Thanks to COVID-19, we know what that feels like, don't we?

Jesus always liked fellowship. He enjoyed time with his friends like we do. But imagine this: you have an all-expense-paid trip to Bali (or Heaven), and instead of hightailing it to the airport, you choose to wait and surprise your friends with a visit first. Maybe Jesus didn't handle goodbyes so well. Or maybe he just really enjoyed hanging out with his friends. Plus: breakfast.

Anyway, there was fish—Jesus told them to cast nets off the right side of the boat—and there was bread. There was a fire and a beach. And a bunch of awesome friends. A pretty perfect breakfast scenario, if you ask me.

Fellowship can be a life-giving thing. Sharing food, drinks, laughs—that stuff matters. I'm lucky: I live with people I enjoy spending time with. Still, I don't think fellowship with friends is something I'll take for granted the way I used to, before COVID.

—BKS

How has fellowship felt different for you in the days of COVID? How will you invite Jesus to breakfast?

WEDNESDAY—EASTER 4

> With great power the apostles gave their testimony to the resurrection of the Lord Jesus, and great grace was upon them all. —Acts 4:33

Stories are powerful. Think of the stories that were read to you as a kid. I loved *The Berenstein Bears* and anything by Dr. Seuss. We never forget stories that help shape the way we see ourselves, each other, and the world.

Jesus was a storyteller. Most of his best teaching is in the form of parables.

We love a true story. When someone shares a first-person account of something life-changing that really happened, we're riveted. Testimonies are one kind of true story.

In the years of the early church, the apostles shared their testimonies with all who would listen. People were drawn to the details of Jesus' death and resurrection. Sure, Jesus' story had a hero, some villains, a mysterious twist, and a happy (albeit bittersweet) ending. What's not to love about that?

But, of course, there was much more. This true story was causing people to believe in a risen Savior, raised to life by the One True God. Churches were forming and growing. Families were living in community, sharing all their belongings and their earnings. The Gospel was living among them, and the apostles kept sharing.

The power and grace in their words and actions brought a new kind of life to people everywhere they went. And you know, there is power in our testimonies too.

—BKS

**What is the story you and God are writing together?
Who needs to hear it?**

THURSDAY—EASTER 5

We know love by this, that he laid down his life for us—and we ought to lay down our lives for one another. —1 John 3:16

Loving someone is willing their good, even if the thing that's good for them isn't the thing you'd choose.

I watched *Forrest Gump* recently. Forrest is a person who loves well. In Vietnam, he runs back into the jungle amid gunfire to save his best friend, Bubba, and pulls out three other soldiers as well.

Forrest's love for Jenny is pretty darn close to unconditional. He rescues her from abuse a number of times over many years, even though she doesn't return his love until her life is nearly through.

Thing is, really loving someone is hard. It requires much more than affection or attraction does. It might go against everything you feel, or think, or want. It might mean you don't swoop in and save the day, even though you could. Sometimes it means getting out of the way, not knowing what happens after that.

Love costs us something.

In the final days and moments of his life, Jesus perfectly modeled that kind of love for us. He laid down his pride, his desires, and ultimately his life, because of love.

—BKS

**What is love asking of you today?
What are some ways you can love those in your life well?**

FRIDAY—EASTER 6

And this is love, that we walk according to his commandments
—2 John 1:6

God's commandments to the Israelites—Torah, which was familiar to most early Christians—were all about living in community, as a set-apart people of God. That meant that living according to Torah would result in both honoring God and respecting neighbor.

For the Jews, loving others—willing their good, even if it hurts—would happen more organically if one was religiously following God's commandments than if one wasn't. In other words, you wouldn't steal from your neighbor, lie to your brother, or treat a stranger badly, because God's law didn't allow for it.

We modern Christians don't follow Torah, though most of what Jesus taught was founded on its principles. Remember Jesus was a student, and later a teacher, in the Temple. So we need look no further than his teachings to understand that loving each other is an imperative of God.

All this talk of Torah comes down to this: we are more likely to act in love toward others if we follow Jesus' teachings than if we don't. And we are more likely to follow Jesus' teachings if 1) we know what they are, and 2) we have spiritual practices that help us live (and love) like Jesus did.

—BKS

Thinking back on the spiritual practices we talked about during Lent, which ones might help shape you to love others as Jesus did?

SATURDAY—EASTER 7

> **And he said to them, Go into all the world and proclaim the good news to the whole creation. —Mark 16:15**

I'll admit that I struggle with evangelism.

I've attended churches where evangelism was like cold-calling strangers, showing up on their doorsteps with the sinner's prayer locked and loaded.

I've also been on the receiving end of evangelism that looked like multi-level marketing—a friend of a friend invites you to coffee, then starts asking you about your walk with God, and tries to sell you on their brand of Jesus.

I find both approaches to be awkward, intrusive, and insulting.

When I was in college, I hung out at the Wesley Foundation, an on-campus Methodist-supported ministry. We had Movie Mondays, where we'd eat pizza and watch a thought-provoking movie, then discuss it with the campus pastor moderating. Those nights were really good for me because I made friends with kids whose faith backgrounds were nothing like mine. Our conversations were organic and honest, full of questions without easy answers. There was no endgame—just talking.

I learned a lot and shared a lot, and the fundamentalist fortress around my brain started to crumble.

To me, that's what evangelism should look like. There is beauty in conversation where beliefs are shared without expectation or condescension. I've had many such conversations that helped me see God, myself, and the world differently. I'm better because of them.

—BKS

What does proclaiming the good news look like to you? How does your belief in God make its way into your conversations with friends and strangers?

SECOND SUNDAY OF EASTER

> Surely goodness and mercy shall follow me all the days of my life, and I shall dwell in the house of the Lord my whole life long. —Psalm 23:6

Psalm 23 is the psalm that gets read a lot at funerals. With good reason. It is comforting to remember that God is with us in our grief, restoring our souls with green pastures and still waters, and walking with us through dark, sorrowful places.

The verse in Psalm 23 that resonates most with me is the last verse, where David asserts that goodness and mercy will follow him as long as he lives.

I believe the goodness David is talking about is God's God-ness.

Suppose life is a cosmic little-league baseball game. God is the parent who cheers for you so loudly it's embarrassing, who puts a band-aid on your knee after you awkwardly slide into third place, and who takes you to Baskin-Robbins after your team loses. That's God's God-ness. It includes things like God's constant presence, companionship, and care.

Mercy here isn't the not getting what we deserve definition we're all familiar with. Instead, mercy is like a soft place to land when we fall. God is with us, ready to catch us and comfort us, not just when we're grieving, but always.

Then there's the idea that I am already dwelling in the house of the Lord and will do so my whole life long.

Because we are already in eternity, we don't have to wait until our mortal existence is through to sit and feast at God's table.

—BKS

**What does goodness and mercy mean to you?
How could you use Psalm 23 in a difficult time?**

MONDAY—EASTER 9

> But Peter said, 'I have no silver or gold, but what I have I give you; in the name of Jesus Christ of Nazareth, stand up and walk.' —Acts 3:6

Once when I was 17, I was driving my Karmann Ghia on a freeway with four passengers. (Four passengers is a lot for a Karmann Ghia.) One of them was my girlfriend-at-the-time, Shannon, who was Pentecostal.

When it was time to slow down before taking an off-ramp, I realized my brakes weren't working. I let everyone know they should hold on, and I used my hand brake to slow our considerable speed. As we approached the traffic light at the end of the ramp—which happened to be red—we had no hope of coming to a stop. So Shannon exclaimed, "Turn green in the name of Jesus!" And it did.

We rounded the turn with a squeal, and I kept working the hand brake. Then before the next light, which was also red, she exclaimed even louder, "Turn green in the name of Jesus!" And it did.

This happened three times.

Now I don't know if it was Shannon's faith, or just lucky traffic-light timing, that allowed us to get home without ever having to come to a complete stop. (We eventually coasted to a stop in my backyard, and my beloved Karmann Ghia was fine, except for its lousy brakes.)

But the thing I continue to be so impressed by is that Shannon's knee-jerk response to a crisis situation was to invoke the name of Jesus. That is never my first response, whether the crisis is mine or someone else's. I do whatever is in my power to make things better. I might pray and call for help. But I don't jump in like Peter did, as if the power of Jesus' name is at my disposal to save the day.

What would happen if I did? What if we all did? How weird would that be?

—BKS

Have you ever invoked the name of Jesus? What happened?

TUESDAY—EASTER 10

The Lord is my shepherd, I lack nothing. He lays me down in green pastures. —Psalm 23:1-2a

In high school I was a Future Farmer of America, raising sheep and goats and working horses in exchange for stall space. The school farm brought in dozens of lambs every year for students to raise, show, and eventually slaughter. I only lasted through one sheep cycle because eventually they'd all have to be butchered and I didn't have the stomach for it.

I should say: almost all had to be butchered. There was a ram at the school farm who was a grumpy so-and-so. He'd haul back and butt everyone who came into his pen. It really hurt, causing almost-grown men to wipe their eyes along with their bruised thighs.

The ram liked me. I don't know why. For months he butted me until he didn't and he'd come when I called him in from the pasture. Maybe it was because I visited him every day, even over school breaks when no one else came around. Maybe the ram knew that if I was there he'd have everything he needed: food, petting, and safety from loud, clumsy boys.

When I was with him, the ram could rest.

When county fair time came around we took all the season's lambs to be shown and sold. We took the ram too. I washed his wool, trimmed his feet, fluffed him up. He didn't appreciate the admiring crowds and was constantly wary, restless, butting the fence to send them scattering.

In the evening, after long days of school and showing and butting, I'd clean his pen, feed him grain, and pluck stuck things from his huge woolly head. Finally he'd lie down in the fresh straw, able to rest. And I would lie with him, my head on his side, the two of us stretched out in the quieting barn.

Sheep don't lie down in their pastures or pens unless their stomachs are full and they feel safe. Neither do we. Those rare times we let down our guard and truly rest, it is because we feel safe and cared for by our Shepherd, whether we realize it or not.

—EOR

**When do you truly rest?
How might you take advantage of God's protection and provision more often?**

WEDNESDAY—EASTER 11

All who obey his commandments abide in him, and he abides in them. And by this we know that he abides in us, by the Spirit that he has given us. —1 John 3:24

At the Last Supper, Jesus leveled the room with some cryptic—and not-so-cryptic—foretellings. The disciples were understandably rattled, so he went on to offer them some reassurances. One of them was this: that they would never be without God's presence because he would ask God to send another Advocate who would never leave them (*John 14:16-17*).

That Advocate is the Holy Spirit. We also know Her as the Helper, the Comforter, or the Paraclete, if you prefer Greek.

The Holy Spirit baffles many Christians.

To some, She is God's fire, reminding us of God's might, power, and mystery.

To others, She is God's breath, reviving and renewing our tired spirits.

I've experienced Her as both, and as neither. She is enigmatic, but if you know God, then you know Her too.

The Holy Spirit reminds us that God abides in us.

There've been times in my life when I've been wracked with grief, or riddled with questions and fears. In those moments, I've felt the Holy Spirit sit with me, listen to me, and cry with me.

Sometimes when worshiping with others, I've felt Her moving through the room, provoking prayer and prompting testimony.

I believe that, while choosing to follow Jesus is an act of our will, it isn't without the involvement of the Holy Spirit, helping us see ourselves as people who need a loving God.

—BKS

**How have you experienced the Holy Spirit?
How did you know it was Her?**

THURSDAY—EASTER 12

> And all of you must clothe yourselves with humility in your dealings with one another, for 'God opposes the proud, but gives grace to the humble.' —1 Peter 5:5b

I used to know a guy who was arrogant. Like really arrogant. His ideas were the best ideas ever thought of. His plans were mind-blowing. He made no mistakes—at least none he ever owned up to. And he made no apologies.

Unsurprisingly, he wasn't nearly as awesome as he thought he was. In fact, a little humility would've gone a long way to earning him the respect he wanted so badly.

We've all known people who are a bit full of themselves. Most of the time, all their boastful talk is an attempt to hide their insecurities, and distract from their failures.

But as someone who is typically a pretty humble guy, nothing gets me riled up like arrogance. And then you know what? I become prideful about my humility, which is the opposite of humble.

Everybody has a kingdom—the part of reality each of us can influence, affect, or control. If you cut me off in traffic, interrupt me when I'm talking, or flirt with my boyfriend, our kingdoms are clashing. This is the stuff that starts wars. If we don't approach those kinds of conflicts with humility, it can get ugly.

I think of it this way: if I'm full of myself, there's no room for things like love, joy, patience, kindness, and the like.

When I refuse to yield my kingdom to God's—and sometimes to yours too—I become the kind of person no one wants to be around. It's life-destroying for you, and for me too.

—BKS

What are ways you can practice being humble? How can you show love to someone who is arrogant (even if that someone is you)?

FRIDAY—EASTER 13

Out of the depths I cry to you, O Lord. Lord, hear my voice!
—Psalm 130:1-2a

I'm a terrible swimmer.

When I was a high school senior, I went with my marching band to Orlando. It was June, it was hot, and it was Florida, so of course, we went to a water park. This one had a wave pool.

First thing, my friend, Susan, headed there and coaxed me to join her. In our zeal to get into the water, neither of us spent the $5 to get a mat, which is essentially a life-saving device for a non-swimmer like me. But no big deal, the waves weren't on anyway, and I had no intention of getting in over my head.

A short time later, the warning horn sounded and the waves started. Sure, I thought about getting out, or spending a little snack money on a mat, but I didn't. I stayed with Susan, bobbing up and down in the moving water.

As the waves got higher, the undercurrent pulled us further out, and pretty soon, I couldn't feel the bottom. The water rolled over my head, wave after wave, and I started to panic. When I couldn't get a breath between waves anymore, all I could do was pray and hope that Susan, or someone, would see me drowning.

Susan got the attention of the hunky lifeguard in the red swim trunks, who blew a whistle, and jumped in. That warning horn sounded again, the waved stopoed, he swam to me, pulled me out, helped me to a chaise, and sat with me while I coughed up what felt like ten gallons of chlorinated water.

I was mortified, having caused a scene barely an hour into our day. But I was alive. (Thanks, Susan.)

Maybe you've been drowning before. If not in water, maybe in debt, or doubts, or depression.

Maybe you couldn't get the words out to ask for help.

Maybe you were just counting on God, or someone, to see you, and help you.

Maybe that's where you are now.

I'd like to say that's the last time I had a harrowing experience in water. It isn't. And it isn't the only time I screamed silently out of desperation, both in and out of water. But every time we call out, God hears us, sees our need, and pulls us to safety.

Sure, we may feel foolish for needing to be saved, but the truth is, we all need saving sometimes.

—BKS

**When have you called out to God in your distress?
How did God respond?**

SATURDAY—EASTER 14

> Jesus also said, 'With what can we compare the kingdom of God, or what parable will we use for it?' —Mark 4:30

There's a picture of me that always reminds me of the Kingdom of God.

Some years ago, my friend and ministry partner Benton (whose contemplations you've been reading) played a concert on acreage behind my house. The event was large, and a bunch of people had worked hard to pull it off, including me. Stage and chairs, equipment and publicity meant weeks of hard work.

Weeks of work, and of prayer. I spent hours asking God for guidance and help, listening to God's responses and silences, and taking in the encouragement God sent me through friends.

That night, when I'd finished welcoming the crowd, I sat down on the ground where I could see both the stage and the audience. Benton was in good voice and spirits, and the crowd was relaxed and happy. Even the weather cooperated, which in Nashville is no small miracle.

During the concert someone snapped a photo of me. It's a terrible image, vanity-wise: I'm tired and sweaty and need a haircut. My bra strap is down my shoulder, and shirt and jeans don't really fit.

In that photo, my face is everything: it beams.

If you saw the picture, you'd have no idea where it was taken, or why, but you'd know what joy and peace and love feel like.

Jesus struggled to explain the experience of living in God's kingdom, so resorted to parables and similes: finding a treasure, recovering something precious you'd lost, the poor fed and prisoners released.

Words can't capture what it's like to live your daily life in constant companionship with God. When your mind is burdened with worry and your body is in pain, your soul has access to a deep well of peace and hope. Your spirit can recharge its batteries with God's power.

Jesus didn't have a camera. So with words he tried to explain the wholeness and peace that came from his connection with God.

Scripture says the crowds didn't really understand.

When I forget what the Kingdom is like, Jesus' words don't always help. But I have that picture, and it's close enough.

—EOR

What helps you remember joy in God's presence?

THIRD SUNDAY OF EASTER

> [The Kingdom of God] is like a mustard seed, which, when sown upon the ground, is the smallest of all the seeds on earth; yet when it is sown it grows up and becomes the greatest of all shrubs —Mark 4:31-32a

It doesn't take much to change someone's day, year, or life. Just a seed really.

I'm not well-versed in chaos theory, but I get the gist of the butterfly effect. You know, the idea that a butterfly moving its wings in Kansas, let's say, can seriously affect weather somewhere far away, like in Japan.

Applied more broadly, chaos theory suggests I can do something seemingly inconsequential that has unintended outcomes, for good or for ill, that I probably will never even know about.

It's like when somebody got the idea to pay for the stranger's latte who was in line behind them at Starbucks. And for hours, people were paying for each other's coffees. Until finally, somebody took the free drink. So in reality, that initial act of generosity materially benefited someone hours later, though sending the kindness down the line certainly brightened many people's day.

Fact is, we sow seeds all the time. A smile. A kind word. An inspirational Instagram post.

On the flip side, a selfish or careless act can ruin somebody's day—or life. None of us lives in a self-sustaining bubble, and our choices impact people we don't even know.

We see it in the viral nature of information and entertainment these days. Made-up facts and offensive antics make their rounds. And people get hurt.

So we can choose to drop seeds that end up growing into resentment, intolerance, self-importance, and the like. Or we can plant seeds that yield goodness, compassion, understanding, and love.

Kinda like the Kingdom of God.

—BKS

How have the actions of a stranger made your day, or life, better? What is something you can do today to sow a seed of kindness?

MONDAY—EASTER 16

> Now the works of the flesh are obvious: fornication, impurity, licentiousness, idolatry, sorcery, enmities, strife, jealousy, anger, quarrels, dissensions, factions, envy, drunkenness, carousing, and things like these. —Galatians 5:19-21a

Paul's listing of the works of the flesh is quite extensive. I referenced the New Revised Standard Version of the Bible, as I usually do, and some of these words required definitions. (*Disclaimer: I went to Webster's, not the original Greek. I also editorialized a little.*)

Fornication is defined as consensual sexual relations between two people who aren't married. Licentiousness is lacking legal or moral restraints, especially disregarding sexual restraints.

Sidebar: Things like purity culture, conversion camps, and objections to sexual education in schools, as well as opposition to contraception, and on and on, have shown churches to be out-of-touch with where society (including many Christians) lands on issues of sexuality across the board. I do agree that sex of all kinds is inherently fleshly, since it involves our bodies.

Surprisingly, sorcery has nothing to do with Harry Potter. It is actually the use of power gained from the assistance or control of evil spirits.

Enmity is positive, active, and typically mutual, hatred or ill will.

Strife is bitter, sometimes violent, conflict or dissension.

Dissension is partisan and contentious quarreling.

And factions are parties or groups, especially within government, that are often contentious and self-seeking.

Carousing makes me think of those westerns I used to watch with my dad as a kid, with barmaids in petticoats, and gunfights in the dusty street. But it is actually less interesting: drinking liquor freely or excessively.

I don't mean to make light of Paul's list of fleshly works. I do mean to point out that it is important to consider what was going on culturally when we read Paul's letters.

Each of them was written to a group of new Christians that was learning how to follow Jesus. Each baby church Paul exhorted had its own challenges, struggles, and learning opportunities. We can't fully grasp what Paul was writing, or why he was writing it, without understanding the historical and cultural context of each letter.

Since I'm not going to do a deep-dive into first-century Galatia to unpack Paul's list, I'd like to offer my own version. This is not meant to replace or challenge Paul's list, but just to remind myself (and maybe you) of some modern life-destroyers common to our 21st-century, American culture. I encourage you to write your own list as well.

Life-destroying works of the flesh aren't always obvious, but here are some that are hard to deny:
- objectifying someone for sexual pleasure
- worshiping things or people that aren't God
- trusting spirits that aren't God's Spirit
- provoking unrest
- obsessing over what someone does or has
- seeking revenge
- bullying
- encouraging intolerance (in all its many forms)
- drinking irresponsibly
- partying to escape being responsible, and
- anything else that destroys life—yours or someone else's.

—BKS

Now...what's your list of life-destroying works of the flesh?

Write it out.

TUESDAY—EASTER 17

> For the Lamb at the center of the throne will be their shepherd, and he will guide them to springs of the water of life, and God will wipe away every tear from their eyes.
> —Revelation 7:17

When we were visiting my grandmother for Christmas a few years ago, she had a massive stroke. My mother, my sister, and I sat in the floor of her bedroom and held her while we waited on the ambulance to arrive. We told her she would be all right. We prayed over her.

I don't know if she had any idea we were there or what was happening. In the days that followed until she passed, I don't know what, if anything, was going through her mind.

I hope she was catching glimpses of the heaven she'd spent her life preparing for. Streets of gold, gates of pearl, the whole nine yards. I hope she was at peace. I believe she is now.

I don't think a lot about heaven. When I was younger, I was scared of death, mostly because I could never be sure if I was headed up, or down, when it was my time to go. But these days, I don't live my life with heaven as my endgame. I mean, I believe I will be with God when this life ends for me, but I have no real concept of what that will be like.

There is one thing I am confident of: there will be no more pain, grief, sorrow, loneliness, depression, illness, or death. God will wipe the last of our tears, and whatever happens after that will be rainbows and roller coasters.

If death is something you worry about, I hope you'll reach out—to us, to a friend, to a therapist, to God. I hope knowing that God is with you <u>now</u> (and not just after your mortal body gives out) gives you courage, peace, and joy as you face this life, and whatever happens next.

—BKS

What about death causes you to worry or to be afraid? What ideas about heaven give you peace?

WEDNESDAY—EASTER 18

Do not rejoice over me, O my enemy; when I fall, I shall rise; when I sit in darkness, the Lord will be a light to me.
—Micah 7:8

I deal with depression.

There've been times I couldn't make even simple decisions, like what to eat, or what to wear. When everything felt so big and consequential that I didn't want to get out of bed. It's like I was wandering in a fog, dragging a ball and chain. No clarity, no hope.

If you've spent any time with me at all, you know that I'm typically an upbeat, optimistic guy. I like to spread hope and share light. When I was at my lowest, the guilt of not being able to be that guy made everything so much worse. The voices in my head were loud and condemning. The shame I felt was debilitating.

There were times when I would literally sit in darkness. But somehow I knew God was with me even then. And over time, a combination of medication, therapy, affirmations, and time with God helped me find my hope again.

Maybe you have had, or are currently having, similar experiences. Maybe you, or someone you love, is living with depression, anxiety, or some other condition that causes a loss of focus, motivation, and hope. If this is you, please tell someone who loves you.

Being depressed doesn't mean your faith is weak, or that your relationship with God is broken.

It means you need to tend to your mental health just as you would your physical health.

Spiritual health, mental health, and physical health are all part of well-being, and they're all connected. Don't be afraid to take action toward your spiritual or mental health. You'd get a broken leg set, after all.

—BKS

If you have felt any of the ways I've described, how will you address the depression and/or anxiety in your life?

THURSDAY—EASTER 19

Hear this, you that trample on the needy, and bring to ruin the poor of the land, saying, 'When will the new moon be over so that we may sell grain; and the sabbath, so that we may offer wheat for sale?' The Lord has sworn by the pride of Jacob: 'Surely I will never forget any of their deeds.' —Amos 8:4-5a, 7

It is not the man who has too little, but the man who craves more, that is poor. —Seneca (*Roman philosopher*)

I understand wanting to be prosperous. I mean, nobody daydreams about sleeping under a bridge when they have a house in the suburbs. And to be clear, there is nothing wrong with money—having it, needing it, or working to earn more of it.

However, God does not owe us, nor promise us, financial prosperity.

I used to own a cafe. Even though I worked really hard and managed my business in a God- and people-honoring way, I didn't get rich making sandwiches and lattes. In fact, I accrued quite a lot of personal debt while trying to keep my cafe from sinking.

I prayed in frustration about my lack of income, and doubted I'd ever get back on my feet. God didn't answer my prayers by wiring thousands to my checking account. But God did help me find the courage and resourcefulness to make different choices, and to dig out of debt.

I think it's nearly impossible to be a person of faith in our prosperity-obsessed culture and not struggle with wanting more. But throughout the Bible, we are warned about the trappings of materialism and greed—that to find out where our treasure is, all we need to do is follow our money.

We are also taught that, instead of chasing wealth, we should seek contentment, and share what we have with those less fortunate. Jesus was clear that holding loosely to what we have, and caring for the poor and the needy, are part of living in God's upside-down kingdom.

Our reward will not likely be a mansion in the Caymans or a flush retirement account. But we will have the peace and joy that come from serving others, the way Jesus did.

—BKS

What is your relationship with money like?
What would happen if you applied God's priorities to your spending habits?

FRIDAY—EASTER 20

For I desire steadfast love and not sacrifice, the knowledge of God rather than burnt offerings. —Hosea 6:6

God likes you.

God smiles when you notice the beauty of the wildflowers that grow beside the road near your house. God chuckles when you tell a dad joke and everyone groans.

God sighs relief when your flight lands safely.

God likes it when you are content.

God sees how you prioritize the needs of your family over your own and would like you to take better care of yourself.

God knows you regret what you said in that argument with your partner, and that you don't know how to take it back.

God isn't surprised that you have anxiety over your finances, and that you wish you'd made different choices in your thirties.

God is on the dreaded phone call with your sister about your mom's memory loss. God knows you haven't slept a solid eight hours since the 90s. God wishes you'd quit that job you hate so much, and trust that the money will come from somewhere else.

God likes the things you think are too different, too weird, too scary, too _____ about yourself. God thinks you're special and spectacular.

God hangs on your every word when you pour out your heart.

God doesn't love you out of obligation and isn't looking for reasons to be mad at you. (God doesn't get mad at you.) God isn't waiting for you to make some grand gesture to prove your love and devotion. (God isn't impressed with grand gestures.)

God just wants your actual love and devotion.

These are all things God wants you to know. Oh, and this: you are God's treasured child.

—BKS

What are some ways you can remind yourself that God treasures you? Why do you think it is so easy to forget?

SATURDAY—EASTER 21

See, the former things have come to pass, and new things I now declare; before they spring forth, I tell you of them.
—Isaiah 42:9

My son, Nick, is smart, focused, and ambitious. He is also funny, levelheaded, and thoughtful. But this isn't really about Nick.

Coming back home to Tennessee for his college graduation—to celebrate my son and his accomplishments—reminded me again that life marches on. Nobody stays the same, and I'm certainly not the same person who left Tennessee here for California in the fall of 2019.

Sitting on my old plaid couch in my old studio apartment in the basement of my parents' house conjures up all kinds of feelings. There's the loneliness I lived with here while struggling in a long-distance relationship for years. There is the stress I had over money, career, and parenting. And the depression that set in when I felt like none of it would ever change for the better.

There's also the banana pudding Mom made for me yesterday, the music I'm still creating with Dennis all these years later, and my kids, who keep making me a proud, happy dad.

Tennessee is home. But moving away has made me appreciate it differently. Like so many country songs tell us, we sometimes see things clearer in the rear-view mirror.

Jobs, relationships, roles, ideas—they sometimes become old things, and then they pass away. We grieve, we grow, and we continue. We start a new career. We vote differently. We learn to smile when we hear someone else's name.

God is always doing new things. Knowing that makes it easier for me to try new things too.

—BKS

**What old things are passing away for you?
What new thing can you celebrate?**

FOURTH SUNDAY OF EASTER

By this we know that we love the children of God, when we love God and obey his commandments. —1 John 5:2

I'm an imperfect parent. But I'd say that's true of every mom and dad I know. Even the most loving, attentive, super-involved parents are actual humans with actual problems.

My mom and dad were also imperfect. They were young when I was born—22 and 25 respectively. They had moved to Nashville only a couple years earlier to start their life together. (I still thank them for making that move from rural Alabama.) They were learning how to be grown-ups, and married, and parents, in the city, all at the same time.

I was a precocious kid. I was creative, overachieving, emotional, and unlike every other boy they'd ever been around. They were winging it, learning as they went, and mistakes were made. But I always knew I was loved. And we all survived.

Thankfully, God offers us all the room we need to discover, fail, recover, and thrive, like the best parents do. Being grown-up children of God means we keep making mistakes, but even though God is a perfect Parent, God does not expect perfection from us.

When we love God, and want to love God better, we do the work to become less self-centered and more others-centered.

We do the work through spiritual practice, and choosing to yield our kingdoms to God's kingdom.

—BKS

What does it mean to you to aspire to be spiritually mature while accepting being imperfect?

MONDAY—EASTER 23

Fight the good fight of the faith; take hold of the eternal life, to which you were called. —1 Timothy 6:12a

I think we agree that Christians are supposed to be fighting the good fight of the faith. But what is it we should be fighting for—or against?

According to a recent survey by Pew Research, evangelical leaders overwhelmingly believe these are the things Christians should be most concerned with:

- Christianity is the one true faith that leads to eternal life (98%)
- The Bible is the Word of God (98%)
- Abortion is usually or always wrong (96%)
- Society should discourage homosexuality (84%)
- Men have a duty to serve as the religious leaders in the marriage and family (79%)

Sit with this list for a minute.

Where did fighting racism land on the list? What about ending gun violence? Where is taking care of the poor, sick, hungry, and homeless? How about caring for our planet-in-crisis?

Seems to me evangelical Christians are picking the wrong fights.

Some of the items on this list just tear people down. Jews, Muslims, and people with spiritual and religious expressions that aren't Christian, are told they practice a lesser faith.

The spiritual standing of women is discounted, and their lives are considered less important than those of their unborn children.

And queer folks are discouraged from...existing...?

We are called to be life-giving, not life-destroying. We can do mighty things if we choose to stand for the things, and people, Jesus stood for. Sadly, those things didn't make the top five in the leaders' list.

—BKS

If you're honest, what would your "top 5 things Christians should be most concerned with" be?
What do you want to do about living them out?

TUESDAY—EASTER 24

Know therefore that the Lord your God is God, the faithful God who maintains covenant loyalty with those who love him and keep his commandments, to a thousand generations.
—Deuteronomy 7:9

Trust doesn't come easily to most of us.

There's the base-level trust I have in my Uber driver, my barber, and my barista.

Then there's the next-level trust I have in most of my friends, my family, and my therapist.

The deepest trust I have is in those closest to me—my best friend, my partner, my parents, and my kids.

Any of these people may test, or even lose, my trust. Could take as little as a bad haircut, or as much as a string of lies or betrayals.

Then there's God.

Trusting God can be difficult when we believe untrue things about God. It's hard to trust a God who we think is easily angered, capricious, hypercritical, and unapproachable.

God gets blamed sometimes for terrible things that happen, like cancer, miscarriages, fatal car crashes, and deadly tornadoes.

Who would trust a God who has hurt them by allowing—or even causing—the pain they suffer?

I wouldn't trust that God.

But God doesn't cause the bad things that happen as a result of our individual or collective choices, or because of we've altered, with our actions, the order God created to sustain us. God also doesn't usually break natural laws on our behalf to swoop in and save the day. But we know that God grieves with us when we suffer, and promises to remain faithful, no matter what we face.

It isn't in God's nature to be anything but good. God is for us, never against us, always faithful, and worthy of our trust. When we suffer, and everyone does, it's easy to forget that.

But here is the bottom-line imperative for us all: Don't believe anything bad about God.

—BKS

When do you find it hard to trust God?
What are some of the bad things you have believed about God?

WEDNESDAY—EASTER 25

You shall put these words of mine in your heart and soul, and you shall bind them as a sign on your hand, and fix them as an emblem on your forehead. —Deuteronomy 11:18

Starting new habits—or changing old ones—is hard. That's because our brains are misers, designed to create shortcuts, and make as many behaviors automatic as possible. This frees up our minds for more pressing matters. Habits are meant to be hard to break.

Changing a habit requires a truly compelling reason, and some serious rethinking. For example, if you say you want to stop watching so much Netflix, but you keep watching because, well, you *like* watching Netflix, then what you really want is to stop *wanting* to watch so much Netflix. Watching Netflix scratches an itch that, once you know what it is, could perhaps be scratched another way, if you decided you wanted it to be.

It isn't enough to just resolve to eat healthier, go to bed earlier, or read your Bible every day. Doing those things must satisfy something in you that needs satisfying—or ease a pain that needs easing.

When we start to realize the benefits of a new behavior, we are more willing and able to spend the mental energy to make it a habit.

We get life-giving habits into our bones with practice. Spiritual disciplines help us form new habits by repeating life-giving behaviors and changing life-destroying thought patterns. But making spiritual disciplines a part of our daily lives starts with seeing a compelling reason to do it in the first place.

—BKS

What spiritual disciplines—prayer, solitude, fasting, for example—are part of your life?
What did it take to make them habits for you?

THURSDAY—EASTER 26

Why do you stand looking up toward heaven? —Acts 1:11b

When the dog is hungry, he sits at my feet, gazing upward, pleading for food.

When the dog wants to go out, he sits at my feet, gazing upward, pleading for me to put on shoes.

Are you sensing a pattern?

Our dog knows most good things come from me so when he wants a good thing, he gazes upward, wordlessly speaking his desires. If he doesn't get fed, or walked, or invited into a lap, he's done all he can.

The dog doesn't have much choice, being thumbless in a world of can openers and leash latches. So he tries to tell me what he wants, then hopes that I'm listening, and undistracted, and inclined to follow through.

You are not a dog. Do you pray as if you were?

Do you gaze up toward heaven, pleading for what you want, hoping God's listening, and undistracted, and inclined to follow through?

After he burst from his tomb, Jesus promised his disciples that they'd get all the power they needed. Then he left them by rising into the heavens.

Instead of doing any of the things they were capable of doing, they just stood there, staring upward.

They'd spent so many years gazing and waiting for him to speak or heal or cook fish that instead of claiming the power he had given them and doing all the good things he'd taught them to do, they just stared up and watched his feet vanish.

Jesus isn't your master like I am for the dog.

Jesus is your master teacher: the one who knows how to do what you want to do, and wants you to know how too.

And God didn't create you to be a dog. God already had dogs. God made you to be glorious, to take the power you've been given and do the great things Jesus is teaching you to do.

Prayer isn't just powerless pleading. Prayer is a conversation with God about the things we are doing together.

—EOR

What glorious things could you do with God's power if you did more than gaze and plead?

FRIDAY—EASTER 27

He placed his right hand on me, saying, 'Do not be afraid; I am the first and the last, and the living one. I was dead, and see, I am alive forever and ever' —Revelation 1:17b-18a

John was on Patmos, a small Greek island in the Aegean Sea, when he had the trippy visions we know from the book of *Revelation*. In this verse at the beginning of his strange journey, John is greeted by a version of the glorified Jesus—with hair like white wool, eyes like fire, feet like bronze, and a voice like an ocean. Don't be afraid, Jesus says, reassuring John that he is alive and holding the keys to death.

Fear is a part of living. Some fears are real and rational—like the one that causes you to head for the basement when the tornado siren sounds. Other fears are based on what-ifs, and worst-case long-shots that aren't actually real.

But here's the thing about fear: whether or not the thing I fear is really real, the fear is absolutely real. And acting—or not acting—out of fear can cause real damage.

In those moments of fear, have you ever heard Jesus say to your spirit, "Don't be afraid"? I have. Many times.

There was the time I lost my last music industry job and I thought my life in music was done. Then again when I signed my divorce papers and I was so afraid that my kids were going to hate me. Also when I walked away from the business I'd built, with a ton of debt, not knowing how I'd pay my bills.

I heard Jesus speaking fear-freeness when I moved to California, grieved a breakup, lived amid a pandemic. And I've heard it every day since.

Don't be afraid.

—BKS

What would you do if you weren't afraid?

SATURDAY—EASTER 28

> Then Moses, the servant of the Lord, died there in the land of Moab, at the Lord's command. —Deuteronomy 34:5

What of you should live beyond you?

There are two major stages of life: building ego and living wisdom.

Stage 1: Construct an "I" for yourself and the world through quests and failures, blacks and whites. Your self-image—success, failure, acclaim, embarrassment—defines you.

Stage 2: Your "I" limits you so you release it, giving your deepest self room to breathe. Resiliency and relationship develop wisdom, patience, kindness, and compassion.

Most people never get to Stage 2. They stop at its edge, clutch their carefully constructed self-image, and retreat.

We think of Stage 1 as The Whole Enchilada. We value success instead of love, wisdom, trust, and peace. Hence war, bad politics, midlife crises, and pitying Moses.

At age 25, Moses finds his role. For 95 years he leads the Israelites through famine and abundance, faith and idolatry, toward a promised land. Moses becomes "MOSES! The Deliverer Of His People!"

Finally, at age 120, he arrives. God tells Moses, "There it is. Everything you've worked for. But you won't get to enjoy it. It's for everyone else." Moses sees all he's worked for, dies, and is buried on its edge.

All those years, all that suffering and frustration, and Moses doesn't get any of the win.

Tragic, right?

Uh, no.

After he took credit for God's work (and God told him off) he realized how much his "I" was getting in the way. He trained a successor and passed his leadership on and kept walking toward his people's good.

There at the edge, he saw his people's future and God's faithfulness. What of him would live beyond him was enough.

You can keep defining yourself in terms of your quests and failures. You can resent all the things you couldn't have, all the Promised Lands you missed out on, and hate yourself (and others) for the mistakes you've made along the way.

Or you can focus on what of you is truly valuable to others, over the long haul, and keep walking toward that.

—EOR

What of your "I" needs to go?

FIFTH SUNDAY OF EASTER

Happy are those who do not follow the advice of the wicked, or take the path that sinners tread, or sit in the seat of scoffers; but their delight is in the law of the LORD, and on his law they meditate day and night. —Psalm 1:1

Am I choosing life?

I can choose to smile at a passerby on the sidewalk, or I can look at my feet as they pass. Did I do a bad thing by not making eye contact? No. Could I have made a positive difference in someone's day if I'd smiled instead? Maybe.

When we are intentional about making choices that make the world better, little by little, we become more like Jesus, and closer to God. Our souls long to be close to God, so making life-giving choices brings us peace and joy. Seems simple enough.

Here's the flipside: We don't intentionally make life-destroying decisions most of the time. It's the little self-centered choices we make that get us in trouble after a while. And because we don't always know how our choices impact other people, we sometimes do more damage to our bodies, marriages, kids, friendships, and spirits than we realize.

When we make choices that are life-destroying, we create distance between us and God. Then our souls start sticking to other things or people, while in search of that soul-satisfaction we're missing. Eventually, we can find ourselves far away from God, utterly dissatisfied with everything.

When I choose to smile at a stranger, I add light to the world, simply by making that choice.

The more we make life-giving choices—big and small—the more it becomes second-nature to us. Before long, we're all habitually smiling at strangers on the sidewalk.

How cool would that be?

—BKS

What is one small life-giving choice you can make today?

MONDAY—EASTER 30

> I am confident of this, that the one who began a good work among you will bring it to completion by the day of Jesus Christ. —Philippians 1:6

I don't tend to leave things unfinished.

Unless you count the many song lyrics I've started over the years that were never completed or set to music. Or the stage musical I started writing a few years back. Or the tv shows I got bored with. Or the books...

Okay, maybe I sometimes start things I don't finish. But it's rare that I flake out on a commitment I've made to someone who isn't me. I rarely back out of a co-writing session, a video chat, or dinner plans. I pride myself on being a reliable friend, a dependable co-worker, and a good son and dad. I never like feeling as though I'm letting someone down.

Thankfully, whether I follow through or not, God always does.

Paul reminds the early Christians in Philippi that God has started a good work in them. Exciting things are happening, and there's momentum for even greater things. Then he assures them that the work God is doing will be completed before Jesus returns. Because God isn't one to ever leave a project undone.

Like with the Philippians, God works with us, in us, and among us, to accomplish great things. But it is our participation—our willingness to be the hands of feet of Jesus—that gets things done. We are required to show up, and follow through.

We choose to work with, and against, God all the time. But when we yield our kingdoms to God's, we can count on the inspiration, strength, courage—whatever is required—do the thing God is asking us to.

—BKS

What work is God doing among you and your people right now?

TUESDAY—EASTER 31

> Our God is in the heavens; he does whatever he pleases. Their idols are silver and gold, the work of human hands.
> —Psalm 115:3-4

I'm not much of an idolizer. I mean, there are people I've known—in person and from a distance—that I've placed on pedestals. Most of them were musical influences, like Michael W. Smith, Bruce Hornsby, and David Foster. A few were pastor-types and writers, like Scotty Smith and Donald Miller. I also have friends that I look up to for their courage, faith, intellect, and creativity.

It's okay—important even—to have people you aspire to be like, and to learn from. That said, I understand that even the brightest of us is flawed. I can admire Steven Spielberg, Taylor Swift, and Barack Obama, for perfectly understandable reasons. But as brilliant, creative, and influential as they are, they are not worship-worthy.

Because we humans are worshipers by nature, we have sticky souls, always adoring someone or something. Maybe you aren't wowed by a shiny statue, like the Israelites occasionally were. But a golden calf is often disguised as a perfect persona or some other ideal—just as meticulously crafted, but way more breakable.

And what about those who haven't earned our acclaim at all? Celebrities and influencers with little to no discernible talent. Political figures without convictions, who just say what their adoring followers want to hear.

Christian personalities, who peddle Jesus for personal gain. They all get worshiped. And when they disappoint us, we're…surprised…?

Only God is worthy of our reverence, adoration, and worship. No one—no matter how famous, attractive, smart, funny, sexy, or influential—will ever satisfy the longings of your soul, or mine.

—BKS

Who do you idolize?

WEDNESDAY—EASTER 32

> So you have pain now; but I will see you again, and your hearts will rejoice, and no one will take your joy from you.
> —John 16:22

I have always felt conflicted over Jesus 2.0.

When I was a youngster at Fundy Fun Summer Camp, we were shown *A Distant Thunder*, a low-budget eschatological horror flick that scared the bejeezus out of me. The story took place in a post-rapture apocalypse, made up entirely of 1970s horror tropes, and draped in prophetic cliches. (Completely appropriate viewing for 12-year-olds in the woods without their parents, by the way.)

The intent was to scare us all into giving our lives to Jesus. All it really did for me was make me terrified of the End Times. All throughout my teens, I was afraid of losing my salvation, missing out on the Rapture, and being left to aimlessly wander a Godless hellscape. All while being chased by cloak-and-dagger baddies, eager to brand me with a 666.

The joy Jesus promised was completely papered over with a propaganda poster that shouted, Fear the Tribulation!

Here are a couple more concerns I have with millennialism.

I know Jesus returning as the Triumphant King is something many Christians long to see. But Warrior Jesus feels out-of-character to me. Kinda like Ninja Gandhi. I just can't seem to wrap my mind around it.

And then there's the blood-washed Bride of Christ (*aka* us) summoned to meet Jesus in the air, while people we know and love are left behind to survive in the aforementioned hellscape. I have a really hard time believing God would really do that.

Jesus never actually said any of these things would happen. But he did promise the disciples they would see him again, and that their hearts would be filled with joy that no one would ever take away.

I believe we will also be with Jesus in the next part of eternity. And I'm confident our hearts, too, will rejoice, free of fear and eschatological fiction.

—BKS

What are your ideas about the Second Coming?

THURSDAY—EASTER 33

Happy is the nation whose God is the Lord, the people whom he has chosen as his heritage. —Psalm 33:12

I was a band geek. Marching band was my nation.

When you are in a marching band, you spend countless hours, standing on asphalt in hundred-degree heat. You learn the music and the drill, and you mentally rehearse the show in your sleep. You take it all very seriously, and you give it more than you thought you could.

You are in it with your closest friends, creating something together that will bring an audience to its feet. You wear your band jacket in the halls of your school with pride—doesn't matter if the jocks look at you like you're nerdy and weird.

You honor those who marched before you, and those who will march in your footsteps when you're gone, by giving your best all the time. And you open your arms to clarinets and trombones alike.

When band is your nation, you always have a home.

What bound me to my band-geek friends was the music, the camaraderie, and the common endgame. The music could've been something else. The goal could've been something else too.

My nation was marching band. Maybe yours was the softball team, or the debate team, or Girl Scouts.

I hope you've had a nation.

We long for that feeling of belonging, of working together toward something big. Not just as kids, but for our whole lives.

We all need more than acceptance. We need belonging.

—BKS

Are you part of a nation?
If so, what is it, and what does belonging feel like? If not, why not?

FRIDAY—EASTER 34

The heavens are the Lord's heavens, but the earth he has given to human beings. —Psalm 115:6

Do you know that old hymn *This Is My Father's World*?

> This is my Father's world
> And to my listening ears
> All nature sings and 'round me rings
> The music of the spheres

Now picture this: You have a sink full of dishes, garbage spilling out of your trash can, crumbs in your carpet, and a bathroom in need of super-scrubbing bubbles. Annoyed, you call your landlord and say, "Hey, can you come over and, like, clean up my place? I mean, technically, it's yours, and it's kinda your fault for renting it to a slob."

Yeah. Ever heard of eviction?

> This is my Father's world
> I rest me in the thought
> Of rocks and trees, of skies and seas
> His hand the wonders wrought

It isn't God's job to clean up after us. God created natural laws that govern things like climate, weather, and seasons.

We know that we can affect those things with our actions. We can harm, or help, our planet.

> This is my Father's world
> He shines in all that's fair
> In the rustling grass, I hear him pass
> He speaks to me everywhere

As people of faith, it seems to me we should lead the charge to care for the earth God gave us. Why do you think it is that we don't?

—BKS

This Is My Father's World was written by Maltbie Davenport Babcock.

SATURDAY—EASTER 35

> God's eye is on those who respect him, whose hope for deliverance is in his love. —Psalm 33:18

I give up.

How many times have you said that, out loud or in your mind?

When has your soul been trapped in a tiny room of worry, shame, or exhaustion?

What has brought you low, pinning you in a fetal position until the weeping ended?

Nothing, ever? Maybe your pain isn't that dramatic, or the challenges you face are mere raindrops on an otherwise sunny window.

"I give up" are the words we scream when we're staring at the empty page where an answer is supposed to be.

"I give up" are the words written on the wall of WTF?!!, the last ones we see when we crash headlong into the inevitable.

When that happens—when our current way of living or thinking is no longer sustainable and we run smack into a reality we don't want to face—we have exactly three choices:

1. To stay there, living in misery and hopelessness or dying by our own hand,
2. To go backwards, pretending that everything is really fine and it will all work out somehow, or

3. To change "I give up" into "I surrender," face the pain, deal with reality, and with God's help, move forward.

Surrender sounds like losing, and loss is our deepest fear. But surrender is really about accepting a situation, acknowledging that if you could fix it on your own you would have, and opening yourself up to the way forward that only God can empower.

When you surrender the idea that you are right, or surrender the idea that you have to figure it out alone, or surrender whatever falsehood got you into that place of despair...

When your hope stops being grounded in your own ability to power through, and starts being centered on the unbreaking, neverending, mighty love of the one God who never leaves you on your own...

That's when a tiny ray of light pierces the wall of darkness, pulls you up off the floor, opens your mind, and makes new things possible.

Surrender is the prerequisite for resurrection.

—EOR

Is there some reality facing you today that calls for surrender, and with it, God's loving, helping hand?

SIXTH SUNDAY OF EASTER

> The Lord God formed the human from the dust of the ground, and breathed into their nostrils the breath of life; and the human became a living being. —Genesis 2:7

99.5% of your body consists of 11 elements: O+C+H+N+Ca+P+S++Mg, along with Na+Cl+K

Soil is also mostly 11: O+C+H+N+Ca+P+S+Mg, plus Si+Al+Fe

Physically, you are separated from soil by only tiny amounts of a few elements.

Mentally, spiritually, emotionally: you and the ground are worlds apart.

Dirt is never more than a physical hodgepodge of elements in varying amounts.

Even on those days when you feel like dirt, you are filled with what even the most fecund field lacks: the breath of the living God.

What is physical is measurable, made up of discernable bits, growing or decaying at a determinable rate. That's the dust of you.

The nonphysical you is spirit and soul, directly connected to the essence of the One living God.

You are a spiritual being living a material existence, subject to the pleasures and tragedies of the physical world but inextricably linked to the majestical, creative, all-encompassing, persistent love that is God.

When you are beaten down and worn out, tired and hurting from hauling around the weight of the world with all its suffering and histories and battles and injustices, remember this:

You are a wonder greater than the stars themselves, for every nonphysical crevice of you is overflowing with God's spirit.

—EOR

A practice to try on:

Breathe.

MONDAY—EASTER 37

> Now there are varieties of gifts, but the same Spirit
> —1 Corinthians 12:4

If you attend a church, then chances are you've taken a spiritual gift assessment. These assessments are kind of like a personality test you might take on Facebook—but written in Christian-ese. They give leaders insight into where you, the member, could be of use to the church.

I'm not knocking these assessments. Anything that helps us better understand ourselves, especially our strengths, is a good thing. But I will say that nailing down what our spiritual gifts are is kind of like nailing down the Holy Spirit. (Good luck with that.)

That's because when we are open to being led by the Spirit, She will often use us in surprising ways.

Sure, if you are a cheerful, outgoing person, welcoming visitors and handing out bulletins is probably a great place for you to serve. If you are good with money, and trustworthy, then maybe you should be the church treasurer.

Serving in your sweet spot is a win for you and for your church.

That said, following Jesus takes us out of our sweet spot on the regular. When we submit to the leading of the Spirit, we learn there is more to us than we thought. We can do things that are only possible with Her help and intervention.

Our willingness and availability become our greatest gifts.

The key to discovering and using your spiritual gifts is allowing yourself to be useful to God. That begins when you practice spiritual disciplines, pray to be a part of what the Spirit is doing in your world, and then go where She leads.

—BKS

Be still and think for a minute before answering:

When has the Holy Spirit been able to change a situation for the better—to bring comfort to someone who needs it, or give someone the aha! moment they've been praying for—because you were there, willing, and available?

TUESDAY—EASTER 38

Now you are the body of Christ and individually members of it.
—1 Corinthians 12:27

For about nine months before moving to California in 2019, I visited various churches around the Nashville area to get a sense of what other churches do. I'd been on staff as a worship leader for ten years, so it had been a long while since I'd just sat in a pew.

The place I enjoyed visiting most was Christ Church Cathedral, an Episcopal congregation downtown.

The building is old, built of stone, complete with gorgeous stained glass and a stunning chancel area.

Feeling of sacredness in the space? Check.

The music at Christ Church is stunningly good. Because their worship is centered around classical music, I wasn't compelled to question their song choices, or rearrange their parts in my head. Their singers are mostly paid professionals and their organist is world-class, so no pitchy altos or bad notes. I was able to rest in their musicianship and just worship.

All of their pastors are smart, thoughtful, appropriately funny, and eloquent. The sermons are poignant, succinct, and thought-provoking. No hour-long ramblings or incoherent illustrations.

And of course, because they are Episcopalian, I was worshiping alongside other LGBTQ+ folks, which made me feel welcome.

While all of those are perfectly good reasons to choose a church, I was surprised by what really attracted me to Christ Church. Being there made me realize that church wasn't really about my tending to my personal relationship with Jesus. Instead, I came to be a part of something bigger than me. I came to share liturgy and Scripture and Eucharist with people who were doing the same thing in churches all over the world.

Being one of many reminded me of something that's easy to forget: worship isn't about me. Or about you. It is about joining our hearts, minds, and voices in the worship of our living God. Experiencing that at Christ Church gave me the perspective I needed to be a more intentional, impassioned follower of Jesus.

—BKS

**Why do you keep choosing your church?
If you're not part of a church, how much of that is about you and not the church?**

WEDNESDAY—EASTER 39

> And you shall know that I am the Lord, when I open your graves...I will put my spirit within you, and you shall live
> —Ezekiel 37:13-14

I watched the first couple seasons of *The Walking Dead* a few years ago. I'm not a fan of horror, but I find zombies to be fairly comical creatures. Just reanimated flesh and bones, incapable of reason, or emotions, driven only by survival.

I've felt like a zombie before.

It was a while after my divorce. I was dealing with running my own business, and the financial stresses that go along with that. I was trying to keep a long-distance relationship together, which left me feeling jealous, lonely, and resentful. I was also co-parenting teenagers (nuff said), and figuring out how I felt about God, myself, and everything else.

I was depressed. Fear, shame, and guilt were deep in my bones. I was stumbling around, doing the daily minimum, but feeling pretty dead inside.

Even in my zombie-like state, with little to give, God gave much to me. Friends kept showing up, reminding me that I was loved, and worthy of love. I rediscovered passions from my youth, like drum corps and roller coasters, that started giving me joy again. I slowly—very slowly—started to trust myself to make life-giving choices.

Prayer, meds, friends and time helped me get through the fog of depression, and to find hope.

God opened my grave. Not in a single, dramatic moment, but over time, in subtle and not-so-subtle ways. The Holy Spirit was close by through that entire season, and through every season since.

If you find yourself in a grave, please talk to someone—a trusted friend, your pastor, a therapist. God's Spirit offers life to you, and to all of us.

—BKS

Have you ever felt like a zombie?
What brought you to that place and how did you find life again?

THURSDAY—EASTER 40

> Cease to do evil, learn to do good; seek justice, rescue the oppressed, defend the orphan, plead for the widow.
> —Isaiah 1:16b-17

Have you ever gotten lost? I have a pretty good sense of direction from behind a steering wheel. But put me on a trail and I can get turned around easily. One of my biggest fears is getting lost in a forest at night. (Heck, the idea of just being in a forest at night gives me the willies.)

It's one of the problems with depending upon GPS, right? We pay attention to the voice and not to the place, which means that we get wherever we're going without knowing how it happened, or how to get home.

Getting lost is especially easy to do when you're not paying attention.

In Isaiah 1, God lays out a case against the people of Judah. They were being rebellious and arrogant. But then, God offers an invitation to them to change, a prescription for finding their way back home.

The six actions that God put before Judah are the same things Jesus taught in the Gospels. They are directions for us to find our way when we've strayed from our True North.

We start by examining our actions and attitudes to see where we veered off-course. We fix what we can, make amends, ask for forgiveness, start again, do better.

We stop defending ourselves and start standing up for the defenseless. That means seeking opportunities to help and serve those disadvantaged, ostracized, bullied, and ignored.

Then we make it a point to pay attention to what's going on with our own souls. What are drawn to that isn't God and why?

There's always a way back home. But first, we have to recognize how lost we are.

—BKS

When have you been lost?
How did you find your way back?

FRIDAY—EASTER 41

To set the mind on the flesh is death, but to set the mind on the Spirit is life and peace. —Romans 8:6

Ever wake up with a thought in your head that pretty much wrecks your whole day? Like a memory of something your ex said to you? Or a thing you read in the news? Or a frustration from work?

I wake up like that and it takes a lot of effort to shake that kind of thought. It comes charged with feelings and a list of *what if*'s a mile long. I usually feel powerless to change the thing I'm thinking about.

But I can change my thoughts.

Now I'm not saying it's easy. But the big problem is that our thoughts become ideas, and then over time they turn up as beliefs.

Once ideas become beliefs, which are just ideas we're willing to act on, they are much harder to change.

Negative beliefs lead us toward depression and anxiety, sometimes even violence and self-harm.

Positive beliefs build our self-confidence, deepen our trust, and allow us to see the best in others and ourselves.

It all starts with what we think about.

To set our minds on the Spirit, there are a few tried-and-true spiritual practices that help: repeating positive affirmations, practicing gratitude, monitoring what we feed our minds, shifting our attention to the needs of others, and of course, asking God for help.

—BKS

What are you thinking about today?

SATURDAY—EASTER 42

If the world hates you, know it hated me before it hated you.
—John 15:18

Go Ducks!

Gryffindor? Me too!

Red Vines forever, Twizzlers never!

Whether you share an interest or a blood line, being part of a community gives companionship and safety. Anywhere your tribe is, you belong. You're home.

Maybe you're a Green Bay Packers football fan. Driving through the land of the Dallas Cowboys you feel out of place and disoriented. You pull into the parking lot of your favorite chain restaurant and are relieved by the familiar signage. Suddenly you spy a Packers bumper sticker and relief turns to joy. Your tribe is here!

Belonging makes us feel like the world's okay. Even when the world isn't okay and we know it.

Jesus' first apprentices had belonged to a large community. They knew the rules, were invited to the parties. Some of them weren't liked very much (we're looking at you, Tax Collector), but they were part of Israel. They belonged. It was home.

When they decided to follow Jesus, Peter, John, Mary, and the rest thought they were still Jews, connected by blood and history. But, as he told them "if the world hates me, it's going to hate you too." As Jesus got hated, his followers lost their community and its companionship and safety. They didn't belong anymore.

When you follow the Way of Jesus, you're going to go against the dominant culture, no matter what your dominant culture is. Following his Way isn't normal, not even in churches, because you wind up putting that allegiance first: above church, above country, above family, above tribe.

Following Jesus changes everything, including where you find home, where you belong.

The day *before* I was accepted into seminary I was living as a Christian in mostly queer culture. Not the day *after*.

I had thought I was adding to my current life. My tribe thought I had become untrustworthy, bizarre, even dangerous.

That's one of the many reasons so many people identify as Christians, but so few follow Jesus wherever he leads. He happened to lead me to seminary and away from the life I knew. It wasn't fun. At all.

And that's why if you do follow him, try to live his way, no matter where you feel like you belong you'd better find your home in the present Kingdom of God.

—EOR

**Where do you find belonging?
What's your real home?**

SEVENTH SUNDAY OF EASTER

So you are no longer a slave but a child, and if a child then also an heir, through God. —Galatians 4:7

I have a good friend who used to say he experienced God as his boss. As long as he was *doing* things for God—and doing them well—then he was in God's good graces. His relationship with God was very much based on what he was willing to do.

So he started and led a ministry for teens at our church. He sang on the worship team every Sunday. He committed to being mentored by our pastor, and even preached a few times. He probably did lots of other things I never knew about.

But after a while, all the doing became exhausting. So he stopped. And without all the doing, he had no longer had a job. Or a boss.

I used to experience God as a cosmic scorekeeper. Like everything I did, or didn't do, was being tracked. My salvation was always touch-and-go. Only God and my scorecard really knew if my soul was eternally secure at any given moment.

Some of us experience God as aloof, faraway, and uninvested. As if we—and our planet— have been abandoned to our own devices.

Others experience the opposite: God as micromanager, with a divine hand in every little thing. Like nothing happens without God's nod of approval.

None of these perceptions of God—or of ourselves—is true.

We are not slaves, working to appease an easily disappointed God. We are not pawns or puppets. We are not unseen, unheard, or unloved. And we are not victims of God's whims or tantrums. It is inconsistent with God's nature to be cruel, capricious, or unjust.

Instead, we are children of a loving Parent. We are cherished, treasured, and deeply loved by God, who desires good things for all of us, and loves us with an unbreakable, everlasting love.

—BKS

How do you experience God?

MONDAY—EASTER 44

> The Lord bless you and keep you; the Lord make his face to shine upon you, and be gracious to you; the Lord lift up his countenance upon you, and give you peace.
> —Numbers 6:24-26

June is *Pride* Month, a celebration of all things queer. For LGBTQ+ people, it's a time to feel empowered. Rainbow flags are flown in public places. There are parties, parades, and high-fives from allies. If you're queer, like me, it's nice to feel seen and celebrated.

Pride also draws bigotry and homophobia out into the open. Some queer folks feel unloved and unsafe. Many are tired of the tensions, tired of hiding who they are to keep peace, and tired of repeating the same conversations.

Sadly, there is a predictable uptick in violence against LGBTQ+ people during *Pride*. And much of it is perpetrated under the guise of defending traditional Christian values—which must grieve God a great deal.

So pride can deal us soaring highs and crushing lows at the same time.

God gave Moses a blessing to give to the Israelites. It's used often as a benediction in Christian worship services.

I'd like to offer my own take on this blessing for all of us misfits—queer or not—as we enter any month of *Pride*:

May God bless and keep you, wherever you find yourself right now.

May you know that God sees you, hears you, knows you, and loves you.

May you feel accepted and embraced by our loving God, as you are.

And no matter what is going on around you, may the peace of God dwell within you always.

—BKS

What blessing would you offer oppressed people celebrating their identity and belonging?

TUESDAY—EASTER 45

Let love be genuine; hate what is evil, hold fast to what is good
—Romans 12:9

Some things that are good, in my opinion: a summer day at Cedar Point, laughing hysterically with a friend, Mom's banana pudding, watching my favorite drum corps perform from the top of the stands on the 50-yard-line, a well-crafted Manhattan, sharing a new song I just wrote for the first time, spaghetti with meat sauce, leading worship from behind a piano, sleeping in, HGTV at the end of a mentally-exhausting day, and hanging out with my kids—anytime, anywhere.

Likewise, here are some things I believe are evil: movies inspired by eschatology, conversion camps, bubble gum on hot asphalt, putting children in cages, voter suppression, most reality tv, Uber's surge rates, white supremacy, slimy food, addiction, mass shootings, traffic, and Christian nationalism.

You may ask: "How do you know what is good and what is evil?"

"Well," I would answer, "it's a carefully-applied algorithm, based on personal experience, research and observation, societal norms, and my gut."

These days, there isn't much that we can all agree is objectively good or objectively evil. Christians can't really claim any authority in that department anymore (if we ever really could) since we can't even agree amongst ourselves.

In Romans 12:9 Paul's telling everyone to be genuine. But then there's the question of what *is* genuine. If I know someone *really* well, I *might* be able to tell if they are being genuine when they say or do something. But really, all I can do is choose to be genuine in my own actions and interactions, and trust that others are choosing the same.

So what does it mean then to let our love be genuine? I think it means we are to love everyone without motive, expecting nothing in return.

And how do you hate what is evil? By staying away from things that make you think badly about yourself, God, or others.

And what about holding fast to what is good? I think that means that you search for, and find joy, hope, and peace—wherever they happen to be—and then you hold onto them with everything you have. Because they are what make life sweet, unexpected, and marvelous.

—BKS

How do you know when love—yours or someone else's—is genuine?

Bonus question: Name ten things you believe are good.

WEDNESDAY—EASTER 46

> I praise you, for I am fearfully and wonderfully made. Wonderful are your works; that I know very well. My frame was not hidden from you, when I was being made in secret, intricately woven in the depths of the earth. Your eyes beheld my unformed substance. In your book were written all the days that were formed for me, when none of them as yet existed. — Psalm 139:14-16

When I was a kid, I was skinny. Really skinny. I had copper hair, freckles, and ears that stuck out a little. I was shorter than most of the kids at school my age. And I was clumsy, ill-equipped for athletics.

I had (and still have) a tic that appeared when I was feeling stressed or anxious. My kindergarten teachers thought I had a learning disability because I couldn't tie my shoes.

But I was smart. I got the nickname "The Walking Dictionary" when I was in second grade. (I've always liked words.) I was also easygoing, optimistic, and eager-to-please (still true).

I was a late-bloomer. I passed for pre-teen, even after I was driving. I was skinny till I turned 30. Now in my 50s, I'm a little overweight and mostly gray.

Why am I telling you all of this?

Each of us is perfectly imperfect. We see our flaws in the mirror. We tell ourselves we aren't _____ enough. But the truth is, we are exactly as God designed us.

I used to want to be anything but different. But my years have taught me that different is beautiful.

Our differences give us reason to shine, and shining is a good thing.

We were wonderfully made and deeply cherished by God even before our first breath. Freckles, tics, and sticking-out ears included.

—BKS

What is a difference about you that you can celebrate today?

THURSDAY—EASTER 47 (ASCENSION DAY)

> So when they had come together, they asked him, "Lord, is this the time when you will restore the kingdom to Israel?" He replied, "It is not for you to know the times or periods that the Father has set by his own authority. But you will receive power when the Holy Spirit has come upon you; and you will be my witnesses in Jerusalem, in all Judea and Samaria, and to the ends of the earth." When he had said this, as they were watching, he was lifted up, and a cloud took him out of their sight. —Acts 1:6-9

"Are we there yet?"

That's the cliché, right? The family is in the car for a long road trip. Less than 15 minutes away from home, little Billy pipes up excitedly with "Are we there yet?" Then, 3.73 days of boredom-inspired questioning later, Dad (who drives the car) snaps at Billy, "Does it *look* like we're there yet?"

Experience informs me that adults ask "are we there yet?" far more often than children.

Is *this* the last mask mandate?

Will my boss *finally* give me that promotion?

Is *this* the year Black folk stop getting killed by police?

Will my kid stop cutting *this* time?

Is *this* the time when you will restore the kingdom to Israel?

Jesus has been driving the rabbinical car for three years. He's been killed, and resurrected, and appeared all over Galilee to demonstrate God's power.

You'd think that by now his followers would have the sense to trust him and his Father. Maybe even start to get a glimpse of the fact that the restoration of Israel as an earthly power wasn't the point.

But they're anxious for the result they long for. They're tired of trying to do the right thing. They're painfully aware of everything they've done wrong up until now, and they're looking to Dad to set everything right so they can just stop and really, really rest.

Aren't we all? At least sometimes?

Jesus gives his unsatisfactory answer: "Does it *look* like we're there yet?" which in first-century Galilee sounds like, "It is not for you to know."

But Jesus isn't snapping at them like Billy's dad. He's reminding them that while they may be focusing on the wrong things and may not know when their desires will be satisfied (if at all), they do not have to simply wait for someone to do something. They have power to act and will have *even more* when the Spirit comes alongside them.

—EOR

Are you underestimating your own ability to effect change or focusing on the wrong kind of change needed?
What do you want to do about that?

FRIDAY—EASTER 48

O Lord, how manifold are your works! In wisdom you have made them all… When you send forth your spirit, they are created; and you renew the face of the ground.
—Psalm 104:24a, 30

Want to know the biggest difference between God and you?

God is never finished creating, and God's creations are never finished being created. Or re-created.

If you put together flour, water, salt, and yeast to make bread, when are you finished creating your loaf?

When is that song you've been working on for 10 years finished?

If you see streaks in the paint you put on the wall yesterday, do you feel like you have to paint the wall again?

It doesn't matter how you answer: you understand what it means to be finished with something. You know what it feels like to think you're finished and then to discover there's more to do.

You live in linear time with material objects that come into and go out of existence. Of course you have markers for "done."

God doesn't seem to have those same markers. You ever notice how at the end of one of the creation stories in Genesis, God comes to the seventh day and rests? God doesn't wash God's hands, put away all the tools, and head to another project. God just rests. Then God creates some more.

When God sends forth God's spirit (*or* God's breath, depending upon your translation), things are created and the face of the ground (*aka* "adamah"—the same word as for humanity) is renewed.

God breaths and we are renewed, re-created.

God sends God's Spirit and we are born again, and again.

—EOR

When you experience renewal—of your strength, focus, determination, hope—what can you do to notice the presence of God's Spirit in the mix?

SATURDAY—EASTER 49

Elijah said to Elisha, "Stay here; for the Lord has sent me as far as Bethel." [...for the Lord has sent me as far as Jericho...for the Lord has sent me to Jericho...for the Lord has sent me to the Jordan...] But Elisha said, "As the Lord lives, and as you yourself live, I will not leave you." So they went down to Bethel... —2 Kings 2:2, 4, 6 (*adapted*)

The best piece of advice I've received in my long life was this: choose your teachers, not your classes.

Sally didn't intend it profoundly: I was a kid and she was talking about college. She was a visual artist—charcoal and watercolor, mainly—and the wife of my mother's ex-father-in-law. I'm not sure I had seen her before then, and I'm not sure I ever saw her after. But for some reason her words stuck with me.

Choose your teachers because human beings teach us more than the subject matter of their expertise.

At the end of the Elijah (teacher) & Elisha (apprentice) passage, Elisha asks Elijah for a double share of his spirit. It's a bold request, a student asking his teacher to make him even better than the teacher himself. Elijah grants it and Elisha continues leading and teaching as Elijah had (but, one presumes, better than Elijah had).

I don't believe Elijah could have refused, because the transfer and amplification of his spirit was based on Elisha's having stuck close over the long, tiresome journey. Elisha literally followed in Elijah's footsteps for years, watching his teacher, listening to his teacher, eating when his teacher did, sleeping when he did.

Because Elisha was a good student, sticking close, taking wisdom when he found it and discarding foolishness when that's what was offered, over time he absorbed Elijah's spirit as well as access to the Spirit that made Elijah great.

Had Elijah been a scoundrel, or unwise, sticking so close to him would have spelled disaster for Elisha. Haven't we all seen disciples of a fool become twice as foolish themselves? But Elisha chose well, so Elijah and experience and God blessed him.

I've added a codicil to Sally's advice over the years: Choose your teachers *but make sure they are learners too*. Good teachers aren't perfect people, but they admit their mistakes *and* learn from them.

I'm grateful for the good teachers in my life, the ones in the classroom as well as the ones who live with me. They've made me better than I could have been without them, and pointed the way to the Spirit by being the people they are.

—EOR

Who has taught you well?
Have you stuck close enough to inherit their spirit?

Made in the USA
Coppell, TX
01 March 2022